Migration Landing Spaces

This book looks at migrant landing spaces, exploring the processes and infrastructures which people encounter as they navigate urban spaces along the central Mediterranean route.

The book argues that there remains a theoretical and practical difficulty in grasping the complexity of migrant arrivals. Migrants are often unsure whether they will stay or leave, their mobility is uncertain. Despite this, they face rigid binaries and categories within administrative policy and planning which tries to pin them down as either permanent or temporary. Drawing on extensive original research in southern Italy, this book suggests that we should instead think of 'landing spaces': parts of the city that work as infrastructures for landing, that allow for an open and dynamic use of the urban space and provide opportunities for encounter and information exchange as migrants consider their next steps.

Combining an ethnographic gaze with insights from urban planning, architecture, geography, social sciences and migration studies, this book invites us to look closer at the interactions between people, practices and places as migrants land in Europe.

Martina Bovo is an architect and postdoc researcher at KU Leuven, with a PhD in Urban Planning, Design and Policy obtained at Politecnico di Milano (Italy). Her research focuses on the territorial dimension of migratory arrival processes, and broadly on urban and welfare policies and ethnographic approaches to urban analysis.

Routledge Studies in Development, Mobilities and Migration

This series is dedicated to the growing and important area of mobilities and migration, particularly through the lens of international development. It promotes innovative and interdisciplinary research targeted at a global readership. The series welcomes submissions from established and junior authors on cutting-edge and high-level research on key topics that feature in global news and public debate.

These include the so called European migration crisis; famine in the Horn of Africa; riots; environmental migration; development-induced displacement and resettlement; livelihood transformations; people-trafficking; health and infectious diseases; employment; South-South migration; population growth; children's wellbeing; marriage and family; food security; the global financial crisis; drugs wars; and other contemporary crisis.

Forced Migration in Turkey
Refugee Perspectives, Organizational Assistance, and Political Embedding
Edited by Berna Şafak Zülfikar Savcı, Ludger Pries, and M. Murat Erdoğan

Migration Landing Spaces
Processes and Infrastructures in Italy
Martina Bovo

For more information about this series, please visit: www.routledge.com/Routledge-Studies-in-Development-Mobilities-and-Migration/book-series/RSDM

Migration Landing Spaces
Processes and Infrastructures in Italy

Martina Bovo

LONDON AND NEW YORK

First published 2024
by Routledge
4 Park Square, Milton Park, Abingdon, Oxon OX14 4RN

and by Routledge
605 Third Avenue, New York, NY 10158

Routledge is an imprint of the Taylor & Francis Group, an informa business

© 2024 Martina Bovo

The right of Martina Bovo to be identified as author of this work has been asserted in accordance with sections 77 and 78 of the Copyright, Designs and Patents Act 1988.

All rights reserved. No part of this book may be reprinted or reproduced or utilised in any form or by any electronic, mechanical, or other means, now known or hereafter invented, including photocopying and recording, or in any information storage or retrieval system, without permission in writing from the publishers.

Trademark notice: Product or corporate names may be trademarks or registered trademarks, and are used only for identification and explanation without intent to infringe.

British Library Cataloguing-in-Publication Data
A catalogue record for this book is available from the British Library

ISBN: 9781032578668
ISBN: 9781032578682
ISBN: 9781003441342

DOI: 10.4324/9781003441342

Typeset in Times New Roman
by Newgen Publishing UK

Contents

List of figures   *vii*
Preface: The pilot book   *ix*

1   Introduction   1
    1.1   A renewed interest on arrival (or landing?)   1
    1.2   A perspective on migration that turns to urban planning, architecture and spaces   5
    1.3   Methodological notes   6

2   Landing as an open-ended process   12
    2.1   From arrival to landing   12
    2.2   Temporality   22
    2.3   Territoriality   31
    2.4   Populations and uses   38
    2.5   Insightful experiences   45

3   Palermo as crossroads in the central Mediterranean route   62
    3.1   The development of the central route   62
    3.2   Palermo, a 'sponge city' and a 'base point'   71

4   Urban spaces as landing infrastructures   84
    4.1   Plural uses, plural spaces   84
    4.2   Geographies beyond planning logics   87
    4.3   The space as physical setting and object of regulation   104
    4.4   How does landing spatialize?   124

vi *Contents*

5   Working perspectives   131
    5.1   Rethinking the city starting from its uses 131
    5.2   Regulatory frameworks, public action and spaces 135

    Closing credits and acknowledgments   144

    Index   *146*

Figures

3.1	The central Mediterranean route and timeline	64
4.1	Spaces of landing for 'those who stay': a look from above	88
4.2	The geography of landing spaces: a walk through	90
4.3	The Ikenga association	93
4.4	The Arci Porco Rosso helpdesk	95
4.5	The public health clinic Aiuto Materno	98
4.6	The Police Immigration Office	101
4.7	The Foro Italico	103
4.8	Plan of the Immigration Office's waiting area	106
4.9	A morning at the Immigration Office	108
4.10	Plan of the Aiuto Materno health clinic	114
4.11	Observations out of the health clinic	115
4.12	Plan of the Arci Porco Rosso helpdesk	119
4.13	A Wednesday afternoon at the Arci Porco Rosso	121

Preface
The pilot book

There is an object that has been an entry key to this work and represented a continuous reference for the discussion on landing: the *portolano* or pilot book. The *portolano* is a nautical tool, a handbook for along-shore navigation used by sailors to approach the coast. If nautical charts – at various scales – guide in the open sea, pilot books give orientation during landing, here indeed sailors may find all kinds of information on the coast. Initially, they were collections of written and drawn experiences, passed from hand to hand and progressively updated by sailors, through drawings and short explanations on the more difficult passages or protected bays, as well as facilities available on land. In the years, these diaries turned into more structured volumes, and today pilot books are among the obligatory tools to have on board. This object has been an inspiration for this work for many reasons; we can here anticipate three of them. First, pilot books involve an experience-based knowledge. These books were in the first-place diaries, where sailors would annotate their experiences of along-shore navigation, written upon direct experience and progressively updated. Until today, together with more standardized editions, they often report authors' direct experience and personal advice; it is still common use, before leaving the harbor, to call a more experienced fellow and write down their notes. This is also what happens in a short story written by Antoine de Saint Exupéry, in *Terres des Hommes* (1939), that expresses very clearly what is meant by 'experience-based knowledge.' A young pilot, who is about to embark in its first intercontinental passenger flight, asks for advice to a more experienced fellow.

He opened the maps I had brought, and we reviewed together the route. What a geography lesson it was! Guillaumet was not simply teaching me about Spain; he made Spain a friend of mine. He didn't talk about hydrography, neither of populations nor of cattle. He didn't introduce me to Sevilla, but to three orange trees located along the borders of a field close to Sevilla: "watch out! Mark them on the map..." And the three orange trees now seemed to be more relevant than the Sierra Nevada. He didn't talk about Lorca, but about a simple farm located nearby Lorca. A living farm. He was talking about the farmer and his wife. Lost in space, at more than one thousand kilometers away, those two people acquired enormous relevance. In a good position, at the feet of the mountain, like guardians in a lighthouse, they were ready to bring rescue to men. In this way, we were bringing back to evidence all those little details that all the geographers of the world disregard.

(ibidem, pp. 12–13)

Here, as in nautical pilot books, what is at stake is a situated knowledge that is usable by others; pilot books lie in the space between accounts of sailors' diaries and manuals for along-shore navigation. Such experience-based and situated knowledge, as we will see, is particularly valuable when applied to deeply complex and unpredictable processes like migration and landing. They, in fact, develop on and produce forms of knowledge that are hardly found in traditional books and maps; in this sense, to study these processes there is a need to draw new maps and manuals starting from what people experience.

Pilot books are useful reference to go back to also because they come from and address 'those who land.' Far from willing to compare sailors and migrants' experience, this focus is interesting because it defines a group of people on the base of their use of the territory – landing – for a certain period of time, and not on pre-defined and fixed categories. In this volume, the interplay between people, places and practices is very evident; they outline a territory accordingly to the use that a precise population makes of it. Starting from landing practices, they describe places. This becomes clear when looking at the maps provided: differently from geographic maps, or touristic ones, the information about the coast is strongly and uniquely related to the use that sailors would make of it. Roads and restaurants are not reported, instead are indicated sea depths of bays, gas or water refill stations within harbors, and their opening hours. Thus, when consulting pilot books, the bond between sailors, landings and places is particularly evident and this turns useful for a work that aims at investigating landing at the interplay between people, practices and places.

Finally, pilot books are meant to orientate newcomers through an unknown coast and land, and they do it in a very open way, they are indeed open and loose handbooks, rather than normative manuals. This represents of course a point of interest when turning to disciplines as urban planning and policy that make an extensive use of 'manuals.' The kind of information offered by pilot books, being it a drawing, a thick description of the coast, a front view, or tips on which bay is more protected from winds, is never normative; it rather provides some tools to take better choices. In an experience as sailing, where external factors remain largely unpredictable, the kind of indications provided by these handbooks always leaves some space to the individual agency. In pilot books, sailors gather information on the most protected bays but won't find instructions on how to behave or react to an unexpected change of weather conditions in those bays. Unpredictability also characterizes other experiences, and this example provides food-for-thought about the kind of knowledge mobilized to support landings. Hence, borrowed from the nautical realm, this object will be an insightful reference to go back to when needing orientation into the concept of landing – in ever-surprisingly ways.

The pilot book that triggered the link to landing as it is discussed in this work was the last hand-drawn *portolano* of Italy, authored by Emilio Delfino in the 1970s. He was a navigator and cartographer, who during summer, with the sloop *Leprotto* and *Excalibur*, would approach and draw the coastline from the sea. He would refine the drawings during winter by visiting the same places from land. At the end of his Portolano d'Italia, we read, "Here ends the Waggoner of the sea coasts of Italy as they do appear when you sayle there alongst from Ventimiglia unto Trieste and around the islands of Sardinia and Sicily actually delineated by Emilio Delfino surveyor."

1 Introduction

Back in 2018, in one of the first lectures at the doctoral School at the Department of Architecture and Urban Studies in Politecnico di Milano, we discussed the clash between the inertia with which the territory and institutions change and the speed of contemporary economic, social and demographic transformations. On the one hand, an increasingly articulated demand of new urban populations and diverse land uses and, on the other hand, the need to organize the city into spaces and services and to redefine categories and tools for its governance. Migration and arrival processes are certainly among the social and demographic transformations that prompt those who study the city and the forms of spatial organization. This book engages with arrival processes by conceptualizing them as landings and by investigating how they spatialize.

1.1 A renewed interest on arrival (or landing?)

Since the beginning of this century, research and literature in the domain of migration and urban studies have highlighted the changing nature of migration processes by stressing their diverse geographical patterns (Black *et al.*, 2010), and the multiple temporalities (Collins, 2017) and subjectivities (Khosravi, 2010) of migrants. Scholars introduced the concept of 'incomplete' or 'liquid' migration (Black *et al.*, 2010) to describe the complex, transitory and temporary patterns of contemporary international migratory processes. Along this multifaceted journey, the process of arrival gains relevance: no longer a punctual moment at the end of a linear journey, but a complex experience that stretches in time and space. In a context where migration regimes are increasingly imposing legal restrictions (Collins, 2012), on a temporal level, arrival is seldomly a short step preceding settlement but in many cases turns into a long wait (Bernardie-Tahir and Schmoll, 2018) that occurs several times along the migratory trajectory. In the last decade, migration movements have reignited public and academic debate in the Mediterranean and European area, which has been witnessing an increase and relevant changes in the amount and nature of the flows crossing it, with the so-called asylum crisis. The latter was above all a crisis of European states in accommodating and literally creating infrastructures for new arrivals. Across the Mediterranean and in Europe, the combination of migratory movements and polycentric interventions of reception, regulation and repression by institutional and non-institutional actors has fueled the discussion on arrival. The urgency of this discussion is witnessed by the amount of research and projects financed on the issue. Only at a European level, within the international and national projects on asylum, reception and integration,[1] many were specifically revolving around terms such as newcomers, arrival and arrival infrastructures.[2] Thus, not only aiming at assessing migration policies around the Mediterranean and Europe, but also specifically addressing the arrival dimension, under different perspectives.

Within the multidimensionality of arrival processes, the territorial dimension plays a very relevant role, not only in terms of what 'migrants do to the city' but also what 'the city does to migrants' (Bontemps, Makaremi and Mazouz, 2018). For the first time in 2016, an International Architecture Exhibition of the Venice Biennale devoted an entire pavilion to the theme of arrival in cities, with the German experience of *Making Heimat: Germany Arrival Country* (Schmal et al., 2016). In research, the gaze of migration studies is juxtaposed with that of urban studies; the research collective Babels, coordinated by Michel Agier, proposes a translocal look at the Mediterranean cities traversed by these movements: Beirut, Lampedusa, Ventimiglia, Calais, London. At a more local scale, Marco Cremaschi writes of the "Spaces and 'Things' of Immigration" (Cremaschi, 2016), emphasizing how, in addition to nations, are places, localities, countries, and cities that change and will continue to do so, if not through planning, through improvisation. Even closer looks begin to raise the issue of arrival spaces and infrastructures (Meeus, Arnaut and van Heur, 2019), putting the notion of the arrival 'neighborhood' in tension. They notice how the geographies and uses that people in the arrival process make of the city often do not follow the logics of ethnic neighborhoods nor even those of urban and social planning but involve spaces with unprecedented forms, actors and rhythms. In European cities, reception plans and facilities proliferated through very different shapes and showed the mismatch between categories used to govern arrivals and organize arrival spaces and the dynamics characterizing these experiences. Train stations, warehouses, beds in museums and sports arenas became arrival infrastructures, much seemed to escape the logic of urban planning and services: the actors in the field, the location choices, the criteria for access and permanence in these centers. Architecture, up to and including interior design, was also being called into play: what does it mean and how do we construct the visibility, accessibility and relationship with the city of these spaces? Stemming from these reflections and questions, and grounding on the Mediterranean and European context, this book investigates the processes of arrival 'starting from places' and from the use that people in the condition of arrival make of the territory, to question its main understanding and reflect on the tools of spatial organization.

The literature on arrival draws from two main streams of research: on the one hand, the theme of the journey (Khosravi, 2010; Fontanari, 2019; Mannocchi, 2019), investigated in migration studies through disciplinary fields such as anthropology, geography and sociology, and on the other hand, the study of the dynamics and spaces of long-term settlement in the territory. The second field is the one that most traditionally intersects urban studies and urbanism; in particular, the latter deals with migratory and arrival processes as they imply a form of settlement in the territory, reflections from which emerge the debate on forms of integration, diversity and multiculturalism, distribution or concentration in space (Vertovec, 2007; Briata, 2019). Within urban studies disciplines, often, the experience of travel, departure, transit or arrival and what precedes settlement is defined as 'ephemeral,' at low intensity and therefore hard to grasp and deal with in the language of urban planning and policies. However, the experience of migratory processes, and in particular the more recent ones involving the Mediterranean, witnesses the importance of another dimension: that which lies between the journey and a long-term settlement, a condition that maintains the open and processual character of traveling but already implies an intense use of territory. Ethnographic and sociological research narrating the migration experience of refugees and asylum seekers report how people on the move often, upon arrival, do not know whether they will be able to stay or will have to leave again, due to political factors, of constantly changing policies, but also factors such as individual, health, work. These uncertain presences do not imply a light use of the territory, but rather a very intense one – so much so that they change the territories themselves, formulating new questions and needs. Spaces and services are used; often these processes also introduce new and different actors on the territory; public spaces are built or re-functionalized. In this sense, some recent works on the topic of transit and arrival put into question their prevailing meanings and appear particularly illuminating. Papadopoulou-Kourkula (2008) describes transit, in the migratory journey, as a condition that can only be defined *ex post* and that implies a sometimes longer-than-expected use of the territory. Meeus *et al.* (2019) point out that each arrival in a new place does not necessarily imply a subsequent permanence but remains open to a new departure. These works, in other words, help shedding light on the condition between the end of a journey and the beginning of a permanent settlement; not surprisingly, it is precisely these contributions that return to the theme of infrastructure and arrival spaces, emphasizing the markedly territorial dimension of these processes.

In continuity with these authors, this work aims at investigating what happens when migrants – especially refugees and asylum seekers – arrive somewhere but do not permanently settle, a condition that is more and more common (Fontanari, 2019) and often prolonged over time. With the aim of putting these experiences under observation and understanding how they prompt the way the city is thought and organized, the work develops around the concept of 'landing' and its spatialization. The choice of this term stems from the need to think of the experience of landing not as punctual, but as processual and open, as well as to address it, even within the field of urban studies, as a self-standing topic. The term 'landing' provides some benefits over 'arrival,' which instead expresses a time (and space)-limited action. Mainly, landing provides a unique combination of a verb and a noun, i.e. a traveling verb and a place noun – landing pad – thus encapsulating the openness of the journey *and* expressing a link to space and its use, which are the core object of investigation of this work. Additionally, in the common imagination and language, the term 'landing' describes a prolonged process; for instance, when talking about the 'moon arrival,' we refer to the act of the rocket touching the ground, while 'moon landing' describes the whole time astronauts were on the moon. In airports, notice boards display the time and gate of arrival, referring to the exact moment the plane reaches the gate; in the same context, landing includes the time and space between the moment the plane touches the ground and walks down the runway to the gate. In both cases, arrival refers to a time-limited action, while landing encloses a prolonged process and use of space.

1.2 A perspective on migration that turns to urban planning, architecture and spaces

This work proposes a perspective on migration that grounds on a spatial gaze; spaces are not only the field where landing is observed but also intended as tools for migration, social and urban policy addressing these processes. The work embeds its conceptual coordinates in space; namely, it investigates landing mainly through its spatialization on different levels. Choosing spaces as entry points to the research is, in the first place, a choice of a point of view. Space is intended in relational terms, as object of interrelations and a sphere of multiplicity, always under construction as a "simultaneity of stories-so-far" (Massey, 2005, p. 34). Theoretically, this implies that we will primarily refer to contributions that investigate landing starting from – even if not solely – its spatial dimension; hence other relevant aspects, such as legal frameworks, are rather intended as background issues. Urban studies research is taken as the main framework; however, we will also draw from the field of migration studies, which significantly contributes to the debate, especially since their 'local' and 'spatial turn' (Scholten, 2014; Glick Schiller, 2015). Empirically, when observing landing spaces, we will put under observation their material consistency, the practices and uses that take place in them, and the institutionalized and normative system of regulation that operates in space, establishing a connection between the material shaping of space and the processes of production, appropriation and use of the same (Arouna *et al.*, 2019, pp. 16–17). We will try to understand landing starting from the material dimension of spaces, through the consistency of walls, doors, floors, tables, shadows, lights, together with an ethnographic attention on smells, sounds, surfaces, objects and bodies. Then, we will have a look on how uses and practices deploy; how actions and interactions make sense of these spaces; and finally, we will detect how these assemblages, of human and non-human actors, and agencies (Latour, 2005), contain 'grain of truth' (de

Leonardis, 2001) on the organizations and institutions that design and rule landing spaces.

The reasons behind the choice of this point of view are at least two: on the one hand, a personal and disciplinary attitude and, on the other hand, the agreement with some scholar's suggestions on how to investigate arrival and migration processes. Regarding the first, I have chosen to use the sensitivity developed through my studies, which lies in between architecture and ethnography and explores the interplay between people, places and practices (Briata and Postiglione, 2020). However, the choice of starting from spaces stems also from the suggestions that scholars give about how to address plural and dynamic processes. A shared invitation emerging from the literature is to deploy a 'phenomenological approach,' one that starts from looking at how and where things happen (Bianchetti, 2016).[3] Particularly, drawing on the dynamic nature and increasingly tangible spatial dimension of arrival processes, many scholars have claimed for a territorial approach to the study of arrival. This place-based approach also relates to the recent 'spatial turn' (Scholten, 2014; Glick Schiller, 2015), in migration studies. Namely, the idea that starting from spaces, from where migrants' agency takes place, may help avoiding the reproduction of nationalism and ethnicism in making research. A place-based approach helps shifting the attention from categories of people to practices, and this "allows for an understanding of how categories, like legal norms and political directives, are translated into actions and, the other way round, of how practices can inform our knowledge about issues, standards and procedures" (Cremaschi *et al.*, 2020, pp. 190–191).[4] Thus, in this work the spatial dimension is a way and a means to 'see,' a lens with a productive value. Looking at landing practices in space reveals patterns and supports arguments, otherwise less detectable, and space is a common ground where to overlap observations and put them in relation.

1.3 Methodological notes

To this aim, the work builds on experience-based and situated knowledge, gathered throughout a fieldwork in the city of Palermo, in southern Italy and at the center of the so-called central Mediterranean route.[5] The research addresses people who are legally defined as 'refugees' and 'asylum seekers' upon arrival on Italian coasts; however, these categories are not extensively used in the work. Although these labels do affect the paths of migrants and often strengthen their condition of uncertainty, the research tried to avoid their use, which often does not mirror the plural nature of landing. Within the timeframe of migration processes occurred between 2015 and 2020, we will use the term 'landing migrants' to refer to those people who still have an open-ended experience, no matter when their actual arrival took place. As Papadopoulou-Kourkoula (2008) suggests, this condition is not defined by duration but by the degree to which a migrant engages with the structures and opportunities in the receiving countries and invests in hopes, money, contacts, and infrastructure to settle properly. This definition includes various groups and nationalities that often share – even more than in the past – landing conditions, practices, and spaces. Here the notion of population aims at focusing on shared practices and uses of urban spaces, rather than on other analytic categories as gender, age, nationality, ethnicity.

As regards the fieldwork activities, they developed around the qualitative observation of landing spaces through the production of maps, drawings and sketches, and qualitative observations on the characters of urban contexts and interiors, on their uses through an ethnographic approach to the field (Cefaï, 2013). The empirical work started in March 2020 and was first developed at a distance, with desk research, several readings, and online interviews. Between July 2020 and October 2020 field work was developed on site. On the base of a preliminary map built through desk research, I conducted three main activities: interviews, site visits and direct observations. The 52 semi-structured interviews addressed migrants, service providers, policymakers, and scholars. I also had the chance to take part to three meetings held by local associations. Interviews mainly followed a snowball mechanism; thus, the main difficulty was to ensure diversification among the collected points of view. This resulted quite complicated in relation to very sound networks of actors, which have been easily reached through snowball mechanism, but would all provide a rather homogeneous standpoint. In this sense, diversifying sources of contacts has helped, some people have been contacted through website and social networks, others through academic references, others through direct encounters. Secondly, after having defined a more precise map of landing spaces, I have visited them all from the outside and some from the inside during interviews. Thirdly,

I have conducted longer direct observations, complemented with field notes and pictures, but also with informal dialogues with a variety of people. Accessing spaces and getting in contact with the main actors involved was harder than expected, and the degree of negotiation unfolded in the different cases already told a lot about them.

Finally, it is worth underlining that the fieldwork was conducted during the peculiar moment of the COVID-19 pandemic. As for many, the outbreak of the crisis has affected this research. Generally speaking, the pandemic has revealed a magnifying glass of material and immaterial dynamics, from the physical organization of spaces to the power relation among involved actors. It has allowed to 'see' things that otherwise would have remained easily unnoticed. In the debate that has emerged across disciplines on the roles undertaken by the crisis, many have reflected on the amplification that it has produced in different fields (Florida, Rodriguez-Pose and Storper, 2020; Mazzucato, 2020), among them also migration. The pandemic has amplified existing conflicts and challenges already set by migrants' landing along Mediterranean routes; this has been proved by the measures adopted to contain and control migrants' movements, such as the quarantine ships in Palermo's harbor, but also by less visible dynamics that have occurred since March 2020. The observation of landing spaces showed how existing conflicts and weaknesses were enhanced; however, it also rendered more visible the capacities of response of certain realities (Bovo, 2023). At nearly three years distance, the feeling is that the COVID-19 outbreak has somehow caused a 'jump forward,' showing in few months what the risks and opportunities of the current situation are. It is now crucial to reflect on the resources we have, to avoid the risks we have foreseen and invest in the opportunities.

Notes

1 Some examples from the European Union are the AMIF (Asylum Migration and Integration Fund) and the sections 'Migration' in the H2020 calls.
2 Some examples are the 'Cities and Newcomers project' (available at this link: www.cosmopolis.be/research/cities-and-newcomers, last accessed on March 23, 2021), the more recent 'H2020 ReROOT. Arrival Infrastructures as sites for integration for newcomers' (available at this link: https://cordis.europa.eu/project/id/101004704/it, last accessed on March 23, 2021), and the 'ESRC AIMEC: Arrival infrastructures and migrant newcomers in European Cities'.

3 At the beginning of the so-called refugee crisis in Europe, Marco Cremaschi organized an intensive workshop with a group of students of the *Cycle d'Urbanisme* at Sciences Po, in Paris in one of the pivot Mediterranean islands and arrival spaces, to 'see' and investigate what was going on (Cremaschi, 2017).
4 Despite its interest, it is worth underlining that a place-based approach does not erase the risk of categorization, since it still implies a choice on group of spaces – and indirectly of populations – to observe.
5 The literature on 'a southern and Mediterranean thought' have been of great inspiration in this sense, among other authors, we can name Franco Cassano (2007), Fernand Braudel (2008) and Edgar Morin (1999).

References

Arouna, M. *et al.* (2019) *Fluchtort Stadt: Theoretische und empirische Zugänge im Forschungsprojekt, Fluchtort Stadt*. Wiesbaden (DE): Springer Fachmedien Wiesbaden. doi: 10.1007/978-3-658-26871-8_2

Bernardie-Tahir, N. and Schmoll, C. (2018) *Méditerranée des frontières à la dérive*. Lyon: Le passager clandestin.

Bianchetti, C. (2016) *Spazi che contano: il progetto urbanistico in epoca neoliberale*. Rome: Donzelli.

Black, R. *et al.* (eds.) (2010) *A continent moving west?: EU enlargement and labour migration from Central and Eastern Europe* (IMISCoe Research). Amsterdam: Amsterdam University Press.

Bontemps, V., Makaremi, C. and Mazouz, S. (2018) *Entre accueil et rejet: ce que les villes font aux migrants*. Lyon: Le passager clandestin.

Bovo, M. (2023) "Access to essential services. Migrants' landing during lockdown," in Armondi, S. *et al.* (eds.) *Cities learning from a pandemic: Towards preparedness*. London: Routledge, pp. 232–243. doi: 10.4324/9781003240983-18

Braudel, F. (2008) *Il Mediterraneo. Lo spazio, la storia, gli uomini, le tradizioni*. Florence: Bompiani.

Briata, P. (2019) *Multiculturalismo senza panico: parole, territori, politiche nella città delle differenze*. Milan: Franco Angeli.

Briata, P. and Postiglione, G. (2020) "Gratosoglio Ground Zero: persone, luoghi, pratiche," in Cafiero, G., Flora, N., and Giardiello, P. (eds.) *Costruire l'abitare contemporaneo. Nuovi temi e metodi del progetto*. Padova: Il Poligrafo, pp. 337–341.

Cassano, F. (2007) *Il pensiero meridiano*. Bari: Laterza.

Cefaï, D. (2013) "Que est la etnografie?," *Persona y sociedad*, 27(1), pp. 101–119.

Collins, F. L. (2012) "Transnational mobilities and urban spatialities," *Progress in Human Geography*, 36(3), pp. 316–335. doi: 10.1177/0309132511423126

Collins, F. L. (2017) "Desire as a theory for migration studies: Temporality, assemblage and becoming in the narratives of migrants," *Journal of Ethnic and Migration Studies*, 44(6), pp. 119–125.

Cremaschi, M. (2016) "Spazi e 'cose' dell'immigrazione," *Quaderni di Urbanistica3 – Inclusione fragile. Migrazioni nei centri minori del Lazio*, 11, pp. 119–125.

Cremaschi, M. (2017) "Luoghi e legami: cosa impariamo da Lampedusa," *Contesti. Città, territori, progetti*, (1), pp. 34–55. doi: 10.13128/contesti-24187

Cremaschi, M. et al. (2020) "Migrants and refugees: Bottom-up and DIY spaces in Italy," *Urban Planning*, 5(3), pp. 189–199.

de Leonardis, O. (2001) *Le istituzioni: come e perché parlarne*. Rome: Carocci.

Florida, R., Rodriguez-Pose, A. and Storper, M. (2020) "Cities in a post-COVID world." Papers in Evolutionary Economic Geography (PEEG) 2041, Utrecht University, Department of Human Geography and Spatial Planning, Group Economic Geography, revised Sep 2020. https://ideas.repec.org/p/egu/wpaper/2041.html

Fontanari, E. (2019) *Lives in transit: An ethnographic study of refugees' subjectivity across European borders*. London: Routledge.

Glick Schiller, N. (2015) "Explanatory frameworks in transnational migration studies: the missing multi-scalar global perspective," *Ethnic and Racial Studies*, 38(13), pp. 2275–2282. doi: 10.1080/01419870.2015.1058503

Khosravi, S. (2010) *"Illegal" traveller, an auto-ethnography of borders*. London: Palgrave Macmillan.

Latour, B. (2005) *Reassembling the social: An introduction to actor-network-theory*. Oxford: Oxford University Press.

Mannocchi, F. (2019) *Io Khaled vendo uomini e sono innocente*. Milan: Einaudi.

Massey, D. (2005) *For space*. Thousand Oaks: SAGE.

Mazzucato, M. (2020) *Non sprechiamo questa crisi* . Bari: Laterza. Available at: www.ibs.it/non-sprechiamo-questa-crisi-libro-mariana-mazzucato/e/9788858142875 (Accessed: September 8, 2021).

Meeus, B., Arnaut, K. and van Heur, B. (2019) *Arrival infrastructures: Migration and urban social mobilities, arrival infrastructures: Migration and urban social mobilities*. Springer International Publishing. doi: 10.1007/978-3-319-91167-0

Morin, E. (1999) "Penser la Méditerranée et méditerranéiser la pensée," *CONFLUENCES Méditerranée*, 28(Hiver), pp. 33–47.

Papadopoulou-Kourkoula, A. (2008) *Transit migration: The missing link between emigration and settlement*. New York: Palgrave Macmillan.

Schmal, P. et al. (2016) *Making Heimat: Germany, arrival country*. Ostfildern (GE): Hatje Cantz Verlag.

Scholten, P. (2014) "The multilevel governance of migrant integration," in Garcés-Mascareñas, B. and Penninx, R. (eds.) *Integration processes and policies in Europe*. Berlin: Springer, pp. 91–108.

Vertovec, S. (2007) "Super-diversity and its implications," *Ethnic and Racial Studies*, 30(6), pp. 1024–1054.

2 Landing as an open-ended process

The introduction of the term landing in this work stemmed from a fortunate coincidence. The experiences of people on the move I encountered were highly plural, hardly predictable and circular in their mobility; many shared a condition of being arrived while not settled. Despite this being clear, I found it hard to explain why I wanted to focus on this condition. At the same time, with some relief from my side, I started reading that some authors shared the same discomfort: how to describe a process through a word that relates to a precise 'moment,' the moment when a person arrives somewhere? When interviewed, Bruno Meeus reported how, when their work on arrival infrastructures was proofread by English natives, they fell over the question of why they were talking about the 'process' of arrival; reviewers would argue that there is only a 'moment' you can arrive. After struggling to explain this to my supervisor, I showed him an article about pilot books and how sailors would use them upon arrival at sea or 'landing.' Far from willing to compare the experiences of sailors to that of migration, I realized that borrowing this term from a different field could indeed be helpful to liberate arrival processes from the 'punctual' character of the term arrival, opening a space for further investigation on the open-ended nature of these experiences. This chapter will explain the benefits of this word, its relationship with the debate on arrival processes and three dimensions that characterize landing and build this theoretical framework.

2.1 From arrival to landing

The introduction of an alternative term remains in continuity with the debate and particularly with those authors that most recently

DOI: 10.4324/9781003441342-2

Landing as an open-ended process 13

problematize arrival processes. If the concept of arrival has been addressed in urban studies since the beginning of the last century, the debate has mostly intended it as the final moment of migration journeys, preceding and leading to long-term settlements. Instead, in the last decade, authors have started problematizing this understanding, at the intersection between urban and migration studies. Re-tracing the main turning points of the debate is a useful exercise to understand the continuities and steps forward of the proposed framework.

2.1.1 Where traveling ends and settling begins

Arrival, as it is mainly discussed today in the European and Western debate, was first addressed at the beginning of the XX century, in the Chicago School of Sociology. Chicago's scholars discussed the nexus between arrival and the city through the lens of Social Ecology (Park, Burgess and McKenzie, 1925). At the beginning of the XX century, when rural-to-urban movements were one of the main forces of urbanization, Burgess (Park, Burgess and McKenzie, 1925) recognized migration as one of the most relevant drivers of metropolitan development. He illustrated the typical expansion of the city as a series of concentric circles, representing successive zones of urban expansion and the types of emerging areas. This approach introduced an idea of separation and specialization of urban areas; the concept of 'zone of transition' stems exactly from here and it is described as the second concentric circle: a "zone of deterioration, 'slums' or 'badlands' with their region of poverty, rooming-house districts, immigrants' colonies (the Ghetto, Little Sicily, Greektown, Chinatown), Black Belt with its free and disorderly life" (Park, Burgess and McKenzie, 1925, p. 56). The Chicago School of Sociology recognized these areas as a double role: they are 'ports of first entry,' and they fulfill the mentioned transition function. Thus, on the one hand, they offer a first point of access to the city, being highly socially and culturally heterogeneous, often experiencing physical transformations, and poverty in public spaces (Bressan and Tosi Cambini, 2011). On the other hand, they support a certain degree of mobility toward other – and hopefully better – neighborhoods; indeed Burgess described the following circle area as a 'second immigrants settlement' (Park, Burgess and McKenzie, 1925) that often hosts the second generation of migrants and that is the region of escape from the slum, 'the Deutschland of the aspiring Ghetto family' (*ibidem*). Despite the XX century mobility has changed, this paradigm has remained valid in some cases. This perspective mainly applies to rural-to-urban migrations still occurring in some parts of the Global South and mainly to movements developing through migration chains. The latter case refers to the connections that migrant groups establish across cities or countries that channel the movements of newcomers. In these cases, migrants often have a predefined destination before departure and aim at arriving in specific cities and neighborhoods. Here, they find established support networks that often ensure an easier socio-spatial transition.

Within this framework, many authors agree on the presence in the city of certain areas that play a crucial role for newcomers, defined as arrival areas or arrival neighborhoods. Broadly speaking, they can be described as urban districts, where the concentration of migrant newcomers corresponds to the specialization of some spaces on arrival and transition. The concept of 'arrival neighborhood' shares some features with that of 'ethnic neighborhoods' and more broadly with questions of socio-spatial segregation. However, against the background of a broad literature on 'ethnic enclaves' (Wilson and Martin, 1982) and discussions on so-called neighborhood effects, the arrival areas perspective expands these debates (Hanhörster and Wessendorf, 2020), by taking into account the complexities of arrival in increasingly diverse arrival areas characterized by the over-layering of ongoing immigration (Vertovec, 2007, 2015a). We may argue that the breaking point of the literature on arrival districts regards their understanding as resourceful areas and not merely as destitute neighborhoods. Much of the debate revolves around the investigation of the potentiality of these areas; paraphrasing Sandro Cattacin in his *Why not 'ghettos'?* (2006), the recent debate on arrival areas seems to question *why not arrival neighborhoods?* The shared invitation involves investigating, acknowledging and not underestimating their role. What is their function for migrants and the city at large? What are the resources that these districts provide to newcomers? How should local actors deal with these parts of the city?

Interestingly, recent contributions not only problematize the two main features attributed to the so-called zones of transition by the Chicago School[1] but also introduce a third feature of arrival areas, namely that of 'resourcefulness' (Schillebeeckx, Oosterlynck and de Decker, 2019). They argue that arrival neighborhoods provide newcomers with a range of functional, social and symbolic resources, which are more accessible than in other parts of the city and that work as drivers[2] and regard different fields. One of them is access to housing (Günther *et al.*, 2019),[3] which often deploys through a residual and secondary private rental market. Referring to the European context and to recent flows, Saeidimadani (2012) and Schillebeeckx *et al.* (2019) argue that most newcomers are forced to depend on a residential private rental market, which in many cases is a sort of residual and 'under the radar[,] secondary housing market,' mostly defined by market forces and specialized in offering low-cost – and often low-quality – housing to newcomers. Importantly, state reception and the housing market also play a major role in the emergence of new arrival areas, for example in urban peripheries, suburbs or even small- and medium-sized towns, where newcomers might be able to access housing solutions (Keil, 2017; Tzaninis, 2019; Gardesse and Lelévrier, 2020). A second aspect that often represents a resource in arrival neighborhoods is the possibility for (self-) employment, often bonded with reciprocal social networks. Also in this case, European field studies show how access to job opportunities through formal market exchange is severely impeded for many newcomers due to a combination of society-wide trends – discrimination, required education levels and political/institutional factors – and neighborhood-related factors – stricter law enforcement and differential exclusions. Reciprocal social networks and places where social networks are formed – community centers, central meeting squares – are often indispensable to gaining access to employment and do not always receive the support they need (Schillebeeckx, Oosterlynck and de Decker, 2019). Biehl (2014) describes the neighborhood of Kumkapı, in the inner city of Istanbul, where informal structures offer migrants – in addition to access to housing – access to employment. Here, the brokering of jobs and housing occurs between long-established migrants and newcomers, also beyond co-ethnic networks (Biehl, 2014; Hanhörster and Wessendorf, 2020). Additionally, public institutions and social infrastructures – such as advice centers or language courses – within walking distance can play a decisive role in the arrival process and further integration of residents (Saunders, 2011, p. 58). Welfare services information exchange and social support, represent a key resource, generated through reciprocal social relationships and redistributive welfare provision. In this sense, the presence of governmental and non-governmental welfare organizations and spaces[4] plays a crucial role in offering low-threshold access to services and information and sometimes fulfilling an important referral function (Schillebeeckx,

16 *Landing as an open-ended process*

Oosterlynck and de Decker, 2019). Thus, arrival areas can be described as hubs within cities where a concentration of resources for new arrivals can be found. They can provide newcomers with social networks for accessing societal resources as well as housing and work. In addition, they allow ties to migrants' home countries, for instance via existing infrastructures for transferring goods or information such as money transfer agencies, internet cafes etc. (Hanhörster and Wessendorf, 2020).

2.1.2 Can the phases of migrants' journey be defined *a priori*?

At the turn of the century, the changing nature of migration processes has triggered alternative perspectives on migration journeys; particularly, scholars started problematizing the notion of departure, transit and arrival as fixed phases. Migration journeys grow more diversified, and the debate starts recognizing this diversification. Black *et al.* (2010) focus on labor migration from eastern to western Europe and introduce the concept of 'incomplete' or 'liquid' migration to describe the complex, transitory and temporary patterns of contemporary international migratory processes. Referring to the Asia-Pacific area, Collins (2012) underlines how the paradigm of linear migration journeys starting from point A and ending at point B cannot be anymore considered the only form of migration. He reports how already in 2005, the Global Commission on International Migration (GCIM) went so far as to conclude "that the old paradigm of permanent migrant settlement is progressively giving way to temporary and circular migration" (Global Commission on International Migration [GCIM], 2005, p. 31). In this sense, the distinction between departure, transit and arrival becomes more blurred. In migrants' experiences these phases can be distinguished only *a posteriori*, and the definitions of departure, transit and arrival countries are often overlapping. In the Mediterranean, recent historic events and the character of migration regimes, which increasingly use spatial and temporal restrictions, have played a major role in changing the nature of migratory movements and the possibility to clearly define their phases.[5] The research group *Babels* (Border Analysis and Border Ethnographies in Liminal Situations), coordinated by the French anthropologist Marc Agier, has been working on migratory trajectories across the Mediterranean between 2015 and 2018 and has highlighted the dynamic nature of recent migrations. They argue that the points of arrival are to be intended as plural and similar to points of successive transit, rather than unique destinations (Bontemps, Makaremi and Mazouz, 2018); they define migration as a trajectory made of 'pathways and moorings' (Fr. *parcours et ancrages*). Their research activity explores urban realities such as that of Beirut (Dahdah, Puig and Abou Zaki, 2018), an emblematic city of departure, transit and destination, and great work is done around the arrival and transit in Mediterranean islands and border towns (Bernardie-Tahir and Schmoll, 2018).

In the attempt to unpack the plurality of these trajectories, the work of Papadopoulou-Kourkoula (2008) represents a crucial contribution: she focuses on the notion of transit migration and problematizes it. Drawing from an ethnographic and policy analysis work,[6] she unpacks the condition of transit – very little debated despite its growing scale and multilevel impact on states and people. Papadopoulou-Kourkoula (2008) underlines that migration is usually approached through 'static' dichotomies – emigration-immigration, forced-voluntary, regular-irregular and sending-receiving countries. Instead, the reality of migration movements is far more complex and cannot be grasped by such a dualistic approach – for instance, the destination may or may not become the final destination depending on various factors and circumstances. Indeed, this dualistic view hinders an integrated approach, able to link the overlapping phases of the migrant journey to the broader migration process. In her work, she defines transit migration "as the situation between emigration and settlement that is characterized by indefinite migrant stay, legal or illegal, and may or may not develop into further migration depending on a series of structural and individual factors" (*ibidem*, p. 4). Her analysis shows that the outcome of this process is affected "as much by social and policy structures as it is by social networks and other individual factors. Emotions, preferences and physical condition can have as much of an impact as policy frameworks and decisions" (*ibidem*, p. 141). This definition implies some relevant considerations. Settlement is characterized as indefinite: the limit between the moment when the transit ends and it becomes settlement is not defined by duration, but by the degree to which a migrant engages with the structures and opportunities in the receiving countries and invests in hopes, money, contacts and infrastructure to settle properly. Thus, transit migration is not a migrant category, nor a policy area, but a process and a contingency that cuts across various migrant categories – undocumented, asylum seekers, refugees granted asylum, regularized migrants, students and trafficked persons may find themselves in a condition of transit at some point. This also raises a methodological question on how to study transit migration: are people in transit just because they say that they want to move on? And linked to this, how can transit migration be verified, if only retrospectively? Papadopoulou-Kourkoula interviews both cases, migrants who seemed to be 'in transit' and others who seemed to be 'settled,' and in both cases the transit condition is not identified in terms of time, but in terms of the characteristics that define the transit experience – living conditions, access to protection, rights and opportunities in the host country that makes transit migration not only a mental but also an actual condition. After unfolding the fieldwork throughout three different transit territories – Middle East–Turkey–Greece; Maghreb; eastern Europe – Papadopoulou-Kourkoula (2008) highlights the challenges transit migration sets both for individuals and states. As regards the firsts, on the one hand, the transit condition does not allow migrants to completely rebuild their lives in a country likely to be only a temporary stay place, while on the other, since the country may become a place of lengthy settlement, the individual tries to develop ties and integration. Second, she argues that

> the ambiguities of transit migration make it particularly difficult to develop adequate policy responses. Put simply, it is much more difficult to develop policy measures for a population that may or may not settle, than for a population that falls clearly into one of those categories. Furthermore, the extent to which a country is affected by transit migration depends not only on its own policies, but also on the policies developed by other countries. We have seen this chain impact both within the EU, and outside its borders. Ultimately, transit migration is a global phenomenon that needs common policy responses.
>
> (*ibidem*, p. 148)

The mentioned works problematize the definition of migration journeys through distinct phases such as departure, transit, arrival and settlement. Instead, they argue that "whether a particular phase in the migration route is part of the journey or it is part of the arrival is an open question that can only be answered *a posteriori*" (Papadopoulou-Kourkoula, 2008, p. 5).

2.1.3 Arrival as a process

Along these lines, in the last decade, scholars have added a further step in the development of the arrival concept. Hans *et al.* (2019) argue that in the Mediterranean, starting in 2015, we have witnessed a further differentiation of the populations, dynamics and new spaces involved. They recognize this complexity as part of what Vertovec (2015b) defines as 'another important feature of urban diversification.' Meeus *et al.* (2019) referring to the work of Saunders (2011) and to the only focus on the arrival city, argue that "it does not do justice to the diversity of migration trajectories that shape our city today" (*ibidem*, p. 2). Within this multifaceted journey, arrival is to be considered as an intermediate and temporary stopover (Saeidimadani, 2012), where to find stability to move on (Meeus, Arnaut and van Heur, 2019); the concept of arrival is defined in continuity with that of transit, as previously discussed.

In this sense, the work of Meeus, Arnaut and van Heur (2019) represents a relevant contribution to the debate, and they problematize the notion of arrival as the final moment of the migration trajectory and discuss it as a process. They unpack the concept of arrival within three 'politics of arrival': that of directionality, temporality and subjectivity. They argue that, for decades, migration research has assumed a one-way directional understanding of migration, and only in the 1990s, the relationship between migration flows and places has been given more into attention. In this sense, the dimension of the politics of directionality shows how "migration and arrival cannot be socio-spatially 'fixed' – either on the national or on the urban level – but is oriented toward the future, with migrants shooting their relative engagements toward certain places for a variety of reasons over time" (Meeus, Arnaut and van Heur, 2019, p. 5). A second reason for complexity lies in the temporal understanding of arrival; as seen, differently from the past, arrival today does not necessarily refer to settlement and permanence but is often linked to further transit. However, most Western citizenship rights – and anything deriving from them – are strongly rooted in the concept of permanence in a territory. Meeus *et al.* (2019) argue that it prevails "a dichotomy between temporariness and permanence [that] still plays a crucial role in imagining national citizenship rights (permanence) and in the eligibility criteria to obtain these rights (the right to permanence)" (*ibidem*, p. 5). More and more challenged, this dichotomy hampers a nuanced understanding of temporal politics in the process of arrival.[7] The third aspect they address regards the politics of subjectivity, which highlights the diversification of the populations who migrate and how it clashes with the rigidity of the way fluxes are regulated. It points out the tension between the multiplicity of migrants' subjectivities and the categories used by policies with regulating aims. Thus, the emerging argument is that conceptions of migrant arrival as oriented toward settlement within a national territory and within a particular urban space need to be questioned to do justice to the diversity of the migration trajectories that shape our cities today. These arguments have been largely debated and shared and have recently become the ground for the growing stream of literature on arrival infrastructures.

This stream of literature intertwines with a problematization of the concept of arrival neighborhood and an invitation to follow arrival processes however and wherever they take place. As Meeus *et al.* (2019) write, "depending on the trajectories focused on, politics of arrival can be found in historical urban neighborhoods and in smaller cities and towns, in detention centers in peripheral areas, and in the offices of state employees" (*ibidem*, p. 23). In a more recent contribution, the same authors (2020) recall the concept of 'emplacement' (Smith, 2005) to situate the agency of migrants without choosing a particular spatial scale, such as that of the neighborhood, the city or the country. Starting from here, the attention goes to more fragmented arrival spaces, opportunity structures (Hans *et al.*, 2019) or arrival infrastructures (Meeus, Arnaut and van Heur, 2019). To grasp the sociospatial logics of arrival, even when they exceed the neighborhood's limits, Meeus *et al.* (2019) define 'arrival infrastructures' as all those parts of the urban fabric with which newcomers interact at the moment of arrival, through their agencies and competencies of use (Bovo, 2020). The introduction of the infrastructural perspective (Simone, 2004; Hannam, Sheller and Urry, 2006; Blommaert, 2014) allows to shift the gaze from a static understanding of specific urban areas as places of arrival to more nuanced 'channels' that support or prevent mobility, "the politics of arrival can be operationalized in an analysis of how arrival infrastructures select, give direction to and retain or accelerate certain migratory subjects" (Meeus, Arnaut and van Heur, 2019, p. 15). We may argue that, in line with the politics of arrival, the notion of arrival infrastructures allows us to look at migration processes wherever they take place: considering material and immaterial supports, as well as more robust and fluid ones. As they argue,

Landing as an open-ended process 21

"arrival infrastructures comprise of, for example, a variety of housing typologies (including asylum centers and squatting), shops as information hubs, religious sites, facilities for language classes, hairdressers, restaurants, international shipping and call centres" (Meeus *et al.*, 2020, p. 4). These services can be further unpacked into their spatial dimension, the actors involved, the material artifacts they involve – citizenship papers, work/residence permits and medical files – and the procedures that they support. In the face of these robust and permanent infrastructures, there are more fluid ones – often but not necessarily less material. Meeus *et al.* (2019) refer to them as emerging from social infrastructuring practices (Werlen, 1993) and involving a prominent social dimension. They include not only civic support networks, co-national help practices, but also – we can add – 'spatial interstices' (Ambrosini and Fontanari, 2018), i.e. public spaces and other 'spaces of struggle,' where everyday practices support the arrival and mobility of newcomers. In this sense, Meeus *et al.* (2019) suggest an evocative image of the cities as 'platforms of arrival and take-off,' which temporarily support arrival processes. It is along these lines that we can position the discussion on landing. How does this term provide further space to investigate arrival as an open-ended process?

2.1.4 The term 'land-ing' to focus on the openness and spatial dimension of arrival

As it happens in our everyday lives, the capacity to *name* things – from emotions to facts to theoretical issues – is the first step to address them. In the debate on migration, several authors introduce terms of other disciplines to address unexplored concepts. This is the case of the infrastructural perspective proposed by Meeus *et al.* (2019), who borrow the term from linguistic studies.[8] The term landing is used in the aeronautic field and even before that in the nautical field to describe the fact of a boat reaching the coast – or an aircraft touching ground. In these cases, arrival does not happen in a specific moment, but it rather deploys as a process of gradual approach, orientation and knowledge-gain on an unknown territory. Far from aiming at comparing such experiences with those of migration, it is worth underlining some benefits that this term offers. As mentioned, the word landing provides a unique combination of a verb and a noun, i.e. a traveling verb and a place noun – landing pad – thus encapsulating the openness of the journey *and* expressing a link to space and its use. Not by chance, this term is used to describe arrivals when they are prolonged over time or to describe the long and tentative process of approaching a new destination and the first steps in there. In the fields where landing is used over the word arrival, the tools that are used also mirror this processualism clearly: aeronautic maps and pilot books express the need for orientation, describe uncertainty and are never normative handbooks but rather informative ones. Interestingly, the Dutch word *aangeland*, as for the German *angelandet* (Eng. landed), implies a certain degree of randomness and uncertainty, and it describes the situation of 'happening to be' somewhere, without precisely knowing why, nor where or for how long. The idea of arrival and transit as situations that 'happen' to migrants is already present in the recent literature. Drawing from Zigon's (2015) work, Meeus et al. (2020) argue that newcomers can be said to find themselves 'in a situation' that falls upon them on arrival or that they get caught up in, as a constellation of challenges, possibilities and connections. Landing, unlike arrival, includes the term 'land,' making the relation to space explicit. Such a relation is already central in the debate on arrival and using a term that encapsulates it is crucial when turning to disciplines, such as urban studies and architecture, which struggle in grasping the territorial relevance of 'non-permanent' presences on land, as those of newly arrived migrants. This term sheds light on the relation of people, places and practices; by so doing, we will discover that often the geographies of landing are different from the most conventional ways cities are seen. As the territories pictured in pilot books display information that would be of no use for tourists traveling by car – the sea depth, presence of protected bays and the color of lighthouses' light – similarly the way people who are landing use the territory unveils new spaces or different roles that known spaces can undertake. As Pierluigi Crosta (2010) argued 'the territory is the use we make of it,' the word landing is an invitation to investigate what is the territory that those who land 'make use of.' Starting from here, we will now discuss three main dimensions to substantiate the relation of landing to the migration experience.[9]

2.2 Temporality

The journey by land to Karachi is almost 900 kilometers. Taking it would have meant many checkpoints and many people to be bribed, so we decided to travel by air. With the paper I had received

Landing as an open-ended process 23

from UNHCR, I could obtain a ticket. [...] Just before midnight, we arrived in the vicinity of the railway station in central Karachi. Cantt Station was an odd place packed with Iranian, Iraqi and Afghan refugees, together with poor Pakistani migrant workers, petty gangsters, drug dealers, male prostitutes and a sea of beggars. On the eastern side of the railway station, in a triangular block, there were several small, cheap hotels, mostly occupied by Iranian refugees. [...] Room 404 in Hotel Shalimar, a cheap, shaky five-story hotel, became my home for the next eight months.

(Khosravi, 2010, pp. 31–32)

Shahram Khosravi describes his arrival to Karachi, one of the many arrivals he experiences in his 'illegal' travel from Iran to Europe. After a rejection of his Refugee application and a failed contact with a smuggler, he left Karachi for Delhi, "after eight months in Cantt Station, I knew exactly what to do. It was impossible for me to make it to Europe by myself, so I decided to go to India." (*ibidem*, p. 44). In his auto-ethnography, Khosravi (2010) writes about his numerous arrivals in Iran, Pakistan, India and, only finally and randomly, Sweden. Each landing, such as this one, includes a gradual approach to an unknown territory, it requires sometimes to orientate and gain knowledge about spaces, networks, people; as in this case, each landing is characterized by the desire for a new departure, but in fact its temporality remains unknown until the next stop. In his book and in this short passage, Khosravi describes how the temporal dimension of migration journeys depends on a range of different factors: international and national laws, policies and practices but also more individual ones as money availability, networks and knowledge of the system. He mentions places that are constantly hosting newcomers, places where the collective presence of newcomers seems constant in time, although individuals are there only temporarily.[10] These few lines already give an insight into the temporal dimension of landing that takes on different shapes in the debate across urban and migration studies.[11]

2.2.1 Experiencing plural temporalities

Within the diversification of migration processes, in the 2000s, scholars started claiming for an investigation of the new temporalities of migrants. In these years, indeed new concepts such as 'permanent temporariness' (Bailey *et al.*, 2002; Collins, 2012) or 'permanent transience' (Isin and Rygiel, 2007) emerge and problematize the permanent-temporary binary. Collins (2012) argues that research is still largely characterized by an emphasis on permanent migrant settlement. Instead, it should also focus on other forms of temporariness that are becoming increasingly ordinary ways of living in cities.

> Migrants who arrive on temporary permits with specific limitations or restrictions are incorporated into the fabric of urban society in different ways from those who arrive with access to permanent residence, even if the former eventually find a way to remaining long term. In a context where migration regimes are increasingly utilizing such temporal restrictions it behooves geographers and other scholars focused on migration to address these questions conceptually.
>
> (*ibidem*, pp. 321–322)

Temporary migrants, he writes, are included in the study of migration, but questions of temporariness vs permanence are rarely the subject of theoretical inquiry, whose starting point often remains permanent migration. Whereas temporary migration has been a prominent research theme within migration studies with the two broad emphases of guest workers and circular mobility, Collins (2012) sheds light on other subjects whose daily life is indeed constrained by their migration status and discusses the term 'permanent temporariness.' This concept has two dimensions: one is related to the permanently temporary status of these migrants since their arrival, and the other is related to the continual presence of temporary populations in cities, where this presence often ends up being a structural part of the urban environment itself – as Malecki and Ewers (2007) show in the case of labor market for instance. He argues that

> whether we are concerned with exiles, migrants on various kinds of time-limited work permits, international students, undocumented workers and those who overstay the limits of short-term permits, permanent temporariness speaks to the manner in which these individuals are constrained to a greater and lesser degree in their everyday lives.
>
> (*ibidem*, p. 322)

Five years later, Collins (2018) returns to the concept of multiple temporalities in a contribution about the role of desire in migration processes. He argues that "we cannot limit our understanding of migration to singular moment and purely strategically oriented progression" (*ibidem*, p. 9), but rather made of multiple temporalities and rhythms. The work of Vosko et al. on *Liberating Temporariness? Migration, Work, and Citizenship in an Age of Insecurity* (Preston-Dunlop, Vosko and Latham, 2014) provides a useful perspective on the definition of newcomers' temporariness. Starting from the acknowledgment of the institutionalization of temporariness as an acceptable condition for growing numbers of people worldwide, they argue that temporariness is constructed – and sometimes contested. With respect to migration, the permanent/temporary divide is fueled by the enforcement of different entry categories and forms of legal residency status. Moreover, in their emphasis on entry categories, immigration policies increasingly distinguish between the economically desirable – high skill – and the economically necessary – low skill. Among the factors associated with temporariness, Vosko et al. (2014) identify three interrelated but distinct dimensions: policies and practices producing temporariness, artifacts of temporariness and contestations and alternative understandings of temporariness. They show how temporariness is produced by a wide array of policies and practices enacted by states, supranational institutions, corporations and civil society organizations – temporary work programs, security policies and immigration policies. Additionally, there is a range of material and social objects – artifacts – that structure the various registers of temporariness, such as documents – work permits, employment contracts, citizenship papers, security certificates, medical registrations and certificates of language competence – and institutional spaces – detention centers, border crossings; often these artifacts' deployment reveals how temporariness is produced and sustained in time. Vosko et al. (2014) also recognize contestations and alternative understandings of temporariness, through practices of resistance and alternative framings.

These considerations are valid for migration processes and arrivals in the Mediterranean and European context, starting from 2010. The request for asylum is becoming the only way to regularly access European countries (Tosi, 2017) and procedures have increased the amount of population 'in wait,' who have a switched-off status (Bernardie-Tahir and Schmoll, 2018). Fontanari in her *Lives in transit* (2019) explicitly addresses the temporal dimension of newcomers' arrival processes. She develops an ethnographic study of migrants who have received a temporary residence permit in Italy for humanitarian reasons, hailing from Libya and who subsequently undertook secondary movements within the Schengen area. In her work, she shows how much this dimension matters and affects people's life: "the temporary nature of the legal status on the one hand and the fragmented rhythms of daily life on the other hand lead to an experience of time as dilated, hindering the creation of future projects" (*ibidem*, p. 77). Migrants' time indeed is fragmented between waiting, accelerating, queuing, being still, stopping, repeating, stuck within the framework of asylum policies and within the daily temporal restrictions of reception centers, dormitories, public and private services and transport means (Schapendonk, 2012; Brekke and Brochmann, 2015). This leads Fontanari to introduce the concept of 'temporal justice'; she argues that migrants being stuck in this permanent temporariness are deprived of their temporal justice.[12] Additionally, whereas these experiences are typical of the first-arrival time (Griffiths, 2014), her research protagonists are people who have obtained humanitarian or subsidiary protection, and at the time of the research, they had been living in Italy for almost three years. Hence, temporal complexity is not only referrable to the exact moment of arrival but may apply to a longer process after that. Having highlighted the condition migrants undergo, Fontanari highlights the deep contradiction she encountered in the field: on the one hand, the increasing temporariness that characterizes our cities and their populations, not only newcomers – as also Collins (2012) shows; on the other hand, the static approach through which cities are still largely governed and organized, which still largely considers permanence as the only model in the space–society relationship (Pezzoni, 2013).

2.2.2 Problematizing the temporary–permanent nexus

This literature expresses the urge to problematize the binary between permanent and temporary. In this regard, Vosko *et al.* (2014) argue that efforts to solve problems of temporariness mostly still focus on ensuring permanence; in other words, the dominant permanent-temporary binary values permanent over temporary status. Instead, they suggest problematizing the nexus permanent-temporary by 'liberating temporariness.' This concept implies, on the one hand, freeing individuals and social groups from temporariness as an assigned inferior condition, although this might not mean to denote pathways to permanence; on the other hand, a liberation of temporariness itself from the effects of the framings and social structures that render it harmful (Lenard and Straehle, 2012). In this sense, they argue, the notion of liberating temporariness becomes more complicated than simply proceeding to permanence.[13] This highlights the necessity of undertaking

> the difficult intellectual task of reconceptualizing temporariness and permanence so as to liberate both of them. This requires a challenging work on the ground, especially as it entails the risky move of liberating permanence (as opposed to temporariness) as the sole basis of justice, rights, and security (broadly defined).
> (*ibidem*, p. 25)

Taking up the challenge, Latham (2014) continues these reflections in a further chapter in the same volume.[14] He claims that the temporary–permanent binary mirrors a broader distinction between the enduring and the transient – prominently in Western thought, nation-state vs globalization, space of places vs space of flows, as introduced by Castells (1989) – in which the Western society has always favored what was enduring, as a synonym of stability and certainty. Assuming this approach is contradictory in relation to today's mobile world, he retraces the definition of what is permanent and what is temporary. Permanence, in general terms, refers to

> a status or condition where the temporal horizon is assured (by, say, authorities) to go on such that – within the context of individual and collective social fields – continuity is assumed (especially because a termination date is unspecified). The temporary, in contrast, has a horizon that is not assured, because either there is fixed in the future a clearly defined end point[15] or, more abstractly, continuity is not assured[16] and potential end points lie put, at point that will be determinate by authorities, in a future horizon.
> (*ibidem*, p. 198)

This leads Latham to highlight that the two terms are, in the first place, intensely political claims, particularly in a society based on permanence, the non-permanence becomes a means of exclusion. As also Meeus *et al.* (2019) argue, the "dichotomy between temporariness and permanence still plays a crucial role in imaginings of national citizenship rights (permanence) and in the eligibility criteria to obtain these rights (the right to permanence)" (*ibidem*, p. 5). Latham (2014) concludes that liberating temporariness, then, implies insisting on a condition of indeterminacy.

> In this way, the meaning of migration changes so that is no longer simply a new claim on permanence; re-collective action possibly can raise the stakes of the temporary/permanent interaction and attempt to invert questions of status, security, and rights.
>
> (*ibidem*, p. 201)

In the case of arrival, Meeus *et al.* (2019) write that this perspective allows us to understand migrants' claims for employment, housing, education and civic participation without translating these into pathways to permanence, nor ignoring migrants' search for forms of stability. Hence, these contributions, starting from the acknowledgment of the temporal dimension of migration processes, try to problematize the binary between permanence and temporariness, underlining the intensely political claim underpinning this move. They suggest conceptually to liberate temporariness and practically to embrace a condition of indeterminacy.

2.2.3 Grounding the challenge of liberating temporariness

The way reception has been addressed in Europe, starting from 2015 is a clear example of how the temporary–permanent binary was used. Here, reception systems and structures, as well as other services and facilities, often have only provided provisional and 'emergency' answers; or alternatively, they have required proofs of permanence in the long term to be accessed. In this regard, it is worth mentioning the work of Rahul Mehrotra and Felipe Vera on *Ephemeral Urbanism: Cities in Constant Flux* (2016)[17] that explicitly transposes these reflections in spatial terms, in the urban planning and architectural field (Mehrotra *et al.*, 2017). They describe migration as one of the phenomena that introduce diverse temporalities within the urban environment today, and by addressing extreme cases, they offer intriguing insights. Their work draws from a growing concern in the field of architecture and spatial planning, about the temporary nature of certain uses and spaces. Also in these disciplines, indeed, scholars have highlighted that we should pay more attention to the temporal dimension of cities; at the cutting edge of architecture, urban design and regeneration, there is an increasing role of what is temporary, interim, 'pop-up' or 'meanwhile' uses for land and buildings in our urban areas; this reveals a crisis of the concept of permanence (Bishop and Williams, 2012). Mehrotra and Vera (2015) discuss this issue in terms of 'ephemeral urbanism,' analyze a range of extreme conditions of temporary space occupation and argue that the arising distinction between permanent and temporary should not be conceived as a binary but should rather activate a broader understanding of permanence. The premise of their work is that

> in order for cities to be sustainable, they need to resemble and facilitate active fluxes in motion, rather than be limited by static, material configurations. With the focus shifting from being limited to problems of space, to also incorporating factors that consider time. In this context, however, the distinction between the permanent and the ephemeral is not a binary, referring to what remains vs what vanishes.
>
> (*ibidem*, p. 14)

Among different cases of ephemeral urbanism, their work on the Hindu festivity of Kumbh Mela is an insightful example – although it has many differences from arrival spaces, it raises some shared questions on the ability of cities to host diverse temporalities. This festivity every three years gathers millions of people – in 2007 they were 16 million – for only 45 days. The Kumbh Mela is a city with an expiration date, a "choreographically process of temporal urbanization" (*ibidem*, p. 68). Mehrotra and Vera analyze its planning process – the governance, metrics, spatial grid – its deployment – the subunits, roads, bridges, electricity, tents – its social infrastructures, security system and sanitation. Interestingly, what makes such temporary settlement successful is the fact of having a very strong structure, being organized, in terms of management and space, as if it were permanent.[18] Even if apparently there is an alignment between the temporary nature of the problem and that of the solution, the temporary settlement of Kumbh Mela does embed robust systems – and somehow permanent aspirations. The language of the temporary and that of the permanent coexist; temporary needs are not linked to a poor or precarious organization but rather to a very structured management of space and people – usually deployed only for long-term projects. Thus, Mehrotra and Vera ask themselves, how to embed softer, more malleable yet more robust systems in permanent cities. In their own words, "as architects, planners and designers [...] how can we move toward a more adjustable urbanism that is capable of anticipating and hosting the impermanent?" (*ibidem*, p. 85). They argue that from Kumbh Mela we can learn two things: reversibility and openness. Material and immaterial reversibility teaches us that

> rethinking the urban form in a way that understands rhythm is more important than predicting growth [...] A city is a place where adjustment mechanisms are sometimes more interesting to understand and develop than impeccable anticipation strategies implemented [...] in search for a temporary equilibrium, instead of reacting to a permanent state of crisis that [...] has become our contemporary condition by default.
>
> (*ibidem*, pp. 86–87)

Second, drawing from other recent works,[19] they argue that incompletion and spatial-temporal openness are central questions. Such a mega operation received its robustness and resilience exactly from being conceived as an open work, they write that "Kumbh Mela challenges current design and planning trends by demonstrating how improvisation and incompleteness can become fundamental parts in construction" (*ibidem*, p. 403) and introduce the concept of 'incremental design' (*ibidem*, p. 404) as an urbanism able to accommodate diverse temporalities. They conclude that the construction and the disassembly of the city sheds light on the fact that design must incorporate the anticipation of a more nuanced notion of temporality, "in single buildings as it is in master plans, the embracing of change, as an active dimension in spatial production is something that architects and planners need to consider" (p. 405). Hence, assuming a spatial perspective, Mehrotra and Vera not only confirm the prevailing belief of permanence being the constitutive character of cities, but they also discuss how the nexus between permanent and temporary should not be considered as a binary. Through the extreme case of Kumbh Mela, they suggest how temporary needs can be answered through structural and permanent-aspiring solutions. Ultimately, Mehrotra and Vera – as previously Latham (2014) – suggest that problematizing the binary permanent-temporary implies trying to cope with a condition of indeterminacy and openness.

2.3 Territoriality[20]

> I arrived in Italy in May 2011, in Sicily. After I have done the camp in Calabria, in a village… I stay there two years. Then the camp closed […] So I slept outside for five months, I was in Cosenza, but no work. So I called a friend of mine, I knew him from Libya. He was living in Napoli, thus I went to Napoli […] After Napoli? I went to Milano! I knew Milano from Africa! But once in Italy it was not easy to find Milano. I paid a train and the bus, and then I arrived in Milan, in January. Once in the station I slept there. I slept inside a train for one month. […] – Interview with Badu in Milan, April 2014.
>
> (Fontanari, 2019, pp. 85–86)

> This summer during a trip to Sicily, I met a social worker of a reception center in Catania. Together we cleared up a doubt the workers of that center had been having for a while. They would wonder why the few Eritrean who were hosted in the center had arrived with the word 'Palazzi' written on their arms. They couldn't understand and couldn't either ask the hosts since there was no Tigrine mediator. I then explained that Palazzi is the name of a street in Milan, in an area of the city where for more than 30 years now there has been an Eritrean neighborhood; this neighborhood represents a fundamental reference for Eritrean communities. Those Eritreans had the word Palazzi written on their arm because it was the last information they had been given by phone before departing from Libya. Not to forget it, since phones can get out of battery, get confiscated, or lost, they would rely on their skin to keep that vital information.
>
> (translation by the author; Spada and Valentino, 2018, pp. 40–41)

These two testimonies give us an insight into migrants' landings between Africa and Europe through Italy; both stories express the territorial dimension of migrants' landings. In Badu's story, his trajectory changes continuously and he mentions having landed in Libya, then in Sicily and later in other Italian regions and cities; each landing has always remained open to new changes of directions, so that the map of his journey will probably be definable only *a posteriori*. The second story, the experience of social workers in Sicily, explains how each landing is linked to the previous and the next, and how hard it is to deal with translocal trajectories at a local level; landings, despite needing to be addressed locally, can be fully understood only if conceived in the framework of wider migration pathways. In other words, migrants' landing encompasses a translocal dimension, where landings happen in various places, and these places and landings are often strongly bonded.

2.3.1 Experiencing circular mobilities

For decades, assuming the nation-state as the guiding principle that organizes contemporary societies, migration has been understood as 'one directional,' as if it had to do with a jump from one spatial container to another (Schiller, Basch and Blanc-Szanton, 1992; Meeus, Arnaut and van Heur, 2019). This understanding has been deconstructed and problematized by various streams of literature. The first step was undertaken by so-called transnational studies, which underlined how the space of migration deploys both locally and translocally. In the 1990s, scholars started highlighting that migrants carry histories, attachments and legal and social statuses that link them to a range of places; they claimed a conceptualization of migration as operating in a transitional field of networks. It emerged the field of 'transnationalism studies' (Portes, Guarnizo and Landolt, 1999), which started introducing concepts such as transnational social spaces (Faist, 2000), transnational communities (Al-Ali, Black and Koser, 2001) and transnational social fields (Levitt and Glick Schiller, 2004), accompanied by an increasing interest in the multi-directional sending of finances, ideas, goods and emotional labor (Huang and Yeoh, 2007; Baldassar, 2008), and a new turn in the migration and development nexus debate (de Haas, 2005, 2010a; Schiller and Çağlar, 2010). The emerging transnational paradigm (Glick Schiller, Basch and Blanc-Szanton, 1995) criticized the static approach to migration by discussing the interaction between the global and the local levels, focusing on social networks and transnational linkages. This has also fueled a methodological concern in migration studies (Glick Schiller and Wimmer, 2002), which started being criticized for reproducing a nation-state-building effort when taking for granted the migrants' aspiration to settle in a country and the need for integration in a national society (Meeus et al., 2020). More recently, the so-called mobility turn (Cresswell, 2006; Hannam, Sheller and Urry, 2006) helped deconstructing the static perspective on movements in general and on migrations (Fontanari, 2019). The central idea of the new mobility paradigm is to consider mobility as the normal social form of the contemporary global society, questioning the sedentary and static paradigm (Papastergiadis, 2000; Urry, 2000). Accordingly, travel and mobilities are considered no more as just a question of getting to a destination but rather as performances that have their own effect on social life. Mobility, indeed, is a socially produced motion; it is practiced, experienced and embodied in power relations. When referring to migration processes, additionally, Fontanari (2019) highlights we should not forget the actual power relations at play, which shape migrants' trajectories and that are still linked to the role of nation-states. Today, despite shared aspirations for an open and global world, some forces clearly aim at maintaining existing structures, such as nation-states and sovereignty (Ambrosini, 2018), producing the 'global (im-)mobility regime' (Faist, 2013; Glick Schiller and Salazar, 2013). Thus,

> whereas the mobility lens helps overcome the 'methodological nationalism' (Glick Schiller and Wimmer, 2002), it is also important to consider the global power relations that shape migrants' everyday life (Malkki, 1992), for instance defining the different normative categories used in migration policies.
> (Fontanari, 2019, p. 4)

The progressive deconstruction of a linear understanding of migration has more recently interested also the literature on arrival processes (Meeus, Arnaut and van Heur, 2019). Saunders (Schmal *et al.*, 2016) calls for the understanding of migration as a dynamic trajectory, 'a dotted line' (*ibidem*, p. 22); he discusses the multi-scalar emplacement of migrants, whose paths are highly variable and strongly interconnected, support networks almost always exceed the limits of the occupied space and relate to global contacts and similarly processes of transnational trades – mainly regarding revenues sent back to country of origin – are directly linked to migrations (Saunders, 2011). In this sense, the cited ethnographic work of Fontanari (2019) gives an insight into the territorial complexity of migrants' experience, in its local and translocal dimensions. As seen in the case of

Badu, the life stories of the protagonists of her book express 'a multi-directional, fragmented, but constant mobility,' ongoing, repetitive, interrupted and multi-directional movements, without a clear destination. Fontanari introduces the term 'fragmented circuits' "traced within the city, across Italy, and abroad, alternate with points of stasis where the refugees rest and reorient their movements and their dreams" (*ibidem*, p. 119). As for the temporal dimension, these fragmentation and uncertainty build on structural and external factors, such as policies, employment opportunities, economic crisis – also weather conditions in the case of people working in the construction or the agricultural field – and on individual agencies, encompassing social relations, 'collective knowledge' gain, passage through spaces where people and information encounter and exchange. The recent work of Meeus *et al.* (2019) transposes these reflections to the specific experience of arrival:

> migrants' futuring obviously implies a notion of directionality, a 'where to' that is difficult and at least undesirable to fix beforehand and can therefore best be envisaged from the start as multi-directional. The spatial 'end-point' of arrival cannot be socio-spatially 'fixed' – either on the national or on the urban or neighbourhood level – but is always oriented toward the future, with migrants shifting their relative engagements toward certain places for a variety of reasons over time.
> (Meeus *et al.*, 2020, p. 15)

2.3.2 Problematizing the mobile-sedentary nexus

Despite these reflections, the plural territorial dimension of migration journeys still clashes with the prevailing dualistic approach on sedentariness and mobility, which still informs – mostly Western – societies and spaces. Already in 1993, Alain Tarrius claimed for a problematization of the paradigmatic binary mobile-sedentary, which the increasingly nomad and mobile nature of our age forces us to question. Tarrius (1993) calling for the substitution of the term 'immigrant' with that of 'migrant' works on the two binaries between sedentariness-mobility and identity-otherness, linking them to the construction of the urban and the need to keep together individual trajectories with collective destinies. Against the background of the prevailing principle of sedentariness in the public debate and in migration research, he discusses the paradigm of mobility, 'taking seriously' the diverse temporal and territorial experiences of migrant circulation. Assuming this perspective implies understanding the city no more as the place of sedentariness but rather as a crossroads of mobilities, and it means "shifting the gaze from receiving populations, from the centrality of the local, to who lands or transits without really stopping" (*ibidem*, p. 51). He distinguishes between two modalities of socially constructing the city: the first is indigenous, localized and responsible for territorial hierarchies and national policies, and its spatial production is based on 'juxtaposition' and the nation-state sets the rules. The second modality sees cities as crossroads points for populations on the move; this way of construction of the city works through 'superimposition' and the places that are crossed and inhabited are intended as elements of broader territorial networks. Within this framework, he introduces the notion of 'territories of circulation' (Fr. *territoires circulatoires*). He argues that conventionally[21] the approach builds on the first modality, instead assuming a broader and not binary perspective shows that displacement is not the subordinate status of sedentariness. Through the story of Mohamed, a Tunisian migrant reaching France in the 1960s, Tarrius argues that, despite eventually settling in France, he keeps moving in an in-between condition and on a territory of circulation, which continuously links all the points of the migrant journey. Additionally, these territories of circulation do not only represent the stage of people's movements but are also produced and reproduced by them; indeed, the movement itself produces spaces, new social forms in the same places where 'we' risk to keep seeing only indigenous relationships (*ibidem*, p. 59). In other words, Tarrius underlines that problematizing the binary sedentariness-mobility implies acknowledging that sedentariness is not the only constitutive force of the territory. Finally, he argues that the story of Mohamed teaches us that the binary understanding of migration – and its relation to territories – should leave the ground to a ternary approach: "we are no longer the people from *here*, instead *here* there are both *sedentary* (us) and *mobile* (others) populations" (*ibidem*, p. 59). In other words, to fully acknowledge the importance of circular mobility in the construction of the territory, we should stop thinking in terms of 'us' and 'them' but rather focus on the territory and on all the populations, sedentary and mobile, who use it in a certain moment and space. Interestingly, 20 years later, Tarrius (2010) goes back to the concept of territories of circulation and relates it to the more complex territoriality – and temporality – of recent migration processes, particularly addressing the experience of transmigrants. In the last decades, according to Meeus *et al.* (2019), despite a shared acknowledgment of the importance of a multi-scalar emplacement of migrants, a very limited literature analytically and empirically manages to assume and discuss this perspective. In this sense, they underline the importance of three bodies of literature that address this point: first, the literature on multilevel governance – in political sciences, public policy and EU studies – which discusses the divide between the upper and the lower government tiers but remains very much state-centered (Adam and Caponio, 2019). Second, the works on the proliferation of borders and borders control – in political and urban geography – (Mezzadra, 2015) and the literature of the so-called Sanctuary City "can be interpreted as the attempt to rescale migration and refugee policies and practices from national to urban scales," and which potentially "constitute a threat to national sovereignty" (Bauder, 2017, p. 181). Third, recent research on citizenship has pushed the argument beyond formal citizenship questions to more situated and practice-oriented notions of citizenship (Donzelot, 2011).

2.3.3 Grounding the challenge of circular territories

The challenge to overcome the binary between sedentariness and mobility is very clear in the context of recent European arrival processes. An example of this binary[22] is that of so-called transmigrants, namely those people who found themselves in Belgium but planned to cross the border to the United Kingdom. In the public discourse, more than in the literature, this condition has been referred to as 'trans-migration.' Around these people, it grew a discourse of deportability: a proof of their willingness to stay was needed to grant them access to basic services and rights. This shows how much European societies are still grounded on sedentariness, besides mobility is an ordinary and global feature of urban dwellers. This debate was addressed also in terms of urban planning and policy, within the discourse on arrival spaces. In their latest work, Meeus *et al.* (2020) argue that urban planning normative approach, based on the prevailing principle of sedentariness, has a unique and fixed idea of arrival in the nation-state, the broader metropolitan region and the neighborhood. This hinders and constrains the multi-directionality of migrants' futuring vectors. They mention examples of urban planning practices that have caged migrants' multi-directionality, without recognizing the multi-scalar emplacement of their landings. In many European countries, the intention to stay 'forever' and the provision of local 'ties' are requirements for access to affordable or public housing (Schuermans, Schrooten and De Backer, 2019). In the context of the 2020 COVID-19 crisis, roofless people in Flanders had to prove their 'durable ties' to the city in order to gain access to shelters.

Thus, how to acknowledge migrants' multi-directionality and landings' multi-scalar emplacement in planning and policy practices? To answer this question the work of Darling on *Forced migration and the city* (2017) is a relevant reference; relating to research on undocumented migrant rights' campaign in Arizona (Fernandez and Olson, 2011), he underlines that many migrants claimed "for the right to *come and go* more than they were for the right to *come and stay* (Fernandez and Olson, 2011, p. 415);" hence, he argues for an approach able to articulate an openness to mobility. This point is central and helps clarify what the challenge is also in practical terms. On the one hand, embracing the concept of territories of circulation implies conceptually overcoming the binary approach toward sedentariness-mobility, and this is in the first place an intensely political statement. On the other hand, this approach means to think of policies and spaces able to be crossed, not only lowering the access threshold but also allowing an easy exit, not only providing the possibility to come and stay but also that of coming and going. Conditions of accessibility to certain resources cannot be linked, as in the examples above, to the intention of staying 'forever' in the same place; similarly, the organization of spaces – particularly of arrival spaces – should grant the possibility to access and exit freely. For instance, one of the protagonists of Fontanari's work mentions the experience of Italian dormitories, where not only access procedures require a complicated process but also exit is strictly ruled. This openness to mobility has been a major challenge for many support services for newcomers in Europe, starting from 2014. Services addressing newcomers – from reception to legal and health assistance etc. – are organized and based on the idea that users turn sedentary after arrival. Procedures often require a long-term permanence in the same city. Thus, these services face difficulties in providing effective support, due to the unpredictable mobility of migrants. In other words, the way services are organized is still grounded on a linear and local understanding of migration, which renders them inadequate to address mobile populations. To conclude, it is worth sharing an idea discussed by Cosimo Palazzo, at the time Head of the Area Rights, Inclusion and Projects, in the Welfare Department of the Municipality of Milan, during an exchange. Drawing from his experience in dealing with arrivals after 2015, he envisioned a diffused European network of institutional arrival spaces: facilities where people on the move could receive information, basic assistance and language classes[23] – again as a sort of mobility infrastructure. Unlike many existing support services, the proposal of a European network of arrival spaces draws from the opposite principle, namely the acknowledgment of the multi-scalar emplacement of migrants' trajectories and the need to support them.

2.4 Populations and uses

> When I arrive at home in Venice, I try to explain my father why I took the shared car instead of a fast and cheap flight from Berlin, he cannot understand why I travelled ten hours in this modern world of fast travel, above all in Europe thanks to the Schengen Agreement. I explain that the problem was my friend Amal, who could land in trouble crossing the border from Germany to Italy. 'Why?,' exclaims my father. 'There are no controls any more at the internal borders in the Schengen space. I always fly from Venice to Brussels, through Paris, to London, to Barcelona without problem. No one controls me!' I tell him that Amal runs the risk of serious control because of his skin color, and that a border control could bring him trouble [although he holds humanitarian protection] […]. 'But then what is the problem?' And I reply: 'Well, I can explain why […], but do you have enough time to listen to me? It is a long story'.
>
> (Fontanari, 2019, Preface pp. XVIII–XIX)

This is how Elena Fontanari starts her book *Lives in Transit* (2019). This short episode encompasses many of the points we already touched on the previous subsections, the fragmented temporality and mobility of Amal across an apparently open Europe. However, from this preface emerges the nexus between the individuals who migrate, their competencies of use of the territory and the geographies that emerge. Amal, as the other protagonists of Fontanari's book, is a man of 18–40 years old coming from sub-Saharan Africa, who worked in Libya until 2011 when the war started; he fled to Italy, landing in Lampedusa. After more than one year, he gained a humanitarian protection status: a one-year document that allows people to regularly work and live in Italy; due to difficult living conditions he decided to move to a different European country and landed in Berlin; however, every year he must go back to Italy to renovate his permit. Along this trajectory, the conditions of Amal as a migrant subject have changed; both those related to himself as an individual and those imposed by national and international policies – for instance, the categories linked to legal statuses; upon arrival in Italy he was an asylum seeker, after one year and a half a regular migrant, holding a humanitarian protection and so on. The episode tells also how Amal's condition and subjectivity are strongly affecting his competencies of use of the territory; his skin color and his precarious status somehow force him to choose a certain way of traveling rather than another, and he will use certain spaces and services rather than others. These competencies of use are very different from those of Elena. Thus, Amal's subjective condition and his competencies of use outline a geography and a definition of the territory he crosses – in this case of Europe in general – that only partially overlap with that of Elena. Again, his travel from Berlin to Venice highlights streets and highways, which Elena's father could not even imagine.

2.4.1 Diverse populations, uses and territories

This short story exemplifies quite well a third dimension of landing, namely that related to the plurality of populations, uses and geographies that it might encompass. The diversity of migrants' profiles is broadly addressed by ethnographic works on migrant journeys (Khosravi, 2010) and everyday life (Fontanari, 2019). More precisely, these works investigate the topic of subjectivity and argue that in the case of migrants' experience – and especially refugees and asylum seekers – subjectivity should be defined both from internal and external factors and the relation to power structures plays a crucial role. In other words, migrants' profiles not only are different but also change throughout the migration journey, and this depends both on their own agency and – mainly – in relation to the power structures they are caught in. This argument draws on the broader debate on subjectivity: feminist studies and anthropological research define subjectivity as a process (Kristeva, 1982), where the individual plays an active role in coping with power structures. In this sense the boundaries of the subject are never completely established, and hence, there is always a possibility of change. As Butler (1997) stresses, 'subjection' is both about being subordinated by power as well as 'becoming a subject.' Hence migrants

> emerge as historical subjects embedded in political, social, and economic structures, no longer seen only as numbers or judicial categories to be ordered or managed. Refugees, migrants, asylum seekers, are hence illuminated under different light: they appear as women, men, and children with their feelings, desires, and aspirations embedded in overlapping power structures that affect their multiple identities in an ongoing process.
>
> (Fontanari, 2019, p. 7)

The work of Fontanari (2019) helps give an insight into this concept, by unpacking it through ethnographic testimonies; she applies the lens of subjectivity within two levels of analysis: the effects of power structures on refugees' lives and their active role in the construction of the self. She investigates the first aspect through the observation of migrants' feelings, emotions and desires, which are crucial factors in determining migrants' trajectories (de Haas, 2010b; Schapendonk, 2012; Collins, 2018).[24] It emerges that power structures, resulting in control measures and institutional abandonment typical of the current European border regime, affect their process of self-construction and are internalized by migrants who define themselves as constantly 'in transit' and never 'yet arrived' long after their first arrival. Second, Fontanari (2019) explores how migrants (re)act to the same power structures. She observes a multiplicity of practices,[25] intended as 'tactics'[26] (de Certau, 1984), in a continuum between practices of existence and resistance, often coupled with the power of creativity, and she underlines how through these practices migrants negotiate the structural constraints – temporal and spatial. Particularly, against the temporal and territorial dispossession implemented by power structures, migrants put in place practices of re-appropriation of time and space; for instance, through the daily use and appropriation of certain places – as urban parks or public squares – to which they attribute functions and meanings: a bench is a 'bedroom,' a park is a 'home' and a quiet street 'a place to relax' (Fontanari, 2019, p. 222). The literature on subjectivity helps clarify that subjectivity can change, and a person can undergo different and changing conditions, which can be related to diverse competencies and practices, and this is a relevant first issue to keep in mind. Moving from the debate of subjectivity to an urban studies perspective, a useful framework might be provided by the literature on 'populations.' This piece of literature defines urban populations, no more starting from the notion of subjectivity but from that of urban dwellers that share habits and uses in the city; thus, it helps clarify the nexus between people, practices and ultimately places. Martinotti (1993) outlines the coexistence of different and conflicting practices in the use of the city space and relates it to the notion of urban dwellers that have a different relation to time and space. In this sense, he discusses four types of urban populations: residents, commuters, city users and businessmen; this definition aims at enhancing the presence of a plural set of populations that use the city every day, although in very different manners. Pasqui (2008) broadens this definition and describes populations no more as given analytical categories and identities but as a point of view. Basically, by using the term populations, he suggests we should acknowledge the presence of various and varying populations that share, for a certain time and in a certain space, practices of use of the territory. The belonging of people to one population is always multiple – one person might belong to different populations – and is limited in time and space. Populations are defined by 'families of activities or experiences,' such as work-study experiences, experiences of care or of amusement. Researchers, relatives of hospitalized people, commuters and visitors of cultural events, are all – for a certain time and in certain spaces – populations, defined as such because they share practices and ways of using the city. "Each of these families of experience is linked to the others, and all are organized around plural forms of dwelling and moving; since we cannot think of dwelling as being exclusively associated with staying" (*ibidem*, p. 92). This definition of populations helps overcoming the mismatch between fixed labels associated with urban dwellers and their actual dynamic nature. This framework encompasses quite well migrant populations, who do experience complex temporal and territorial conditions, often different from those of other populations and diverse among themselves.

Interestingly, both in the work on subjectivity and populations, practices are central. There is a strong link between individual subjectivities, competencies of use and uses of the city. In this sense, talking about changing subjectivities implies also considering different uses of the city, and the concept of populations – being defined through uses – explains this clearly. Landing migrants, upon arrival, experience different conditions that provide them with different competencies of use of the territory and allow them for certain uses and prevent them from others. Amal's story shows this clearly: he holds a humanitarian permission that would allow him to travel across Europe; however, his skin color would render him more vulnerable than others when facing controls; this leads him to use shared carpooling as a means of transport, rather than the plain. Dahdah *et al.* (2018) underline the capital of use of some Syrian street vendors in Beirut who, thanks to internal – individual skills and knowledge – and to external factors, manage to set a small survival economy, entering the city interstices and rhythms, performing an interesting use of the city. Thus, populations are plural, their competencies of use are plural and so are the practices they perform on the city. Ultimately, it emerges the link to the territory; along these lines, we may argue that the territory represents a support to these uses, or better said, which populations might find a certain degree of plasticity and 'grips,' or resistance and constraint in it. The territory changes with practices, until we can argue that 'the territory *is* the use we make of it' (Crosta, 2010). Crosta (2018) suggests we should think of the relationship between populations and the territory, not as an interaction but as a transformation, where different subjects are actors of this mutual determination and constitute what is called 'local.' This leads Crosta (2018) to raise an interesting point: we always ask ourselves what kind of people use the city, whereas we should question what kinds of cities are used by people. In other words, the plurality of populations – defined as groups of people sharing certain practices for a certain time – and uses also results in a plurality of territories that are defined by these uses. Once again, the territory used and defined by Amal, across his journey to Venice, includes highways, gas stations and small towns between Berlin and Venice. Instead, the same geographical territory would have had a different definition if crossed by Elena's father, it would have probably been made of two airports and taxi stops. The story told by Antoine de Saint Exupéry (*see* Preface) gives a clear insight on this point: the description of Spain he receives is linked to the use he might make of the territory, in case of an emergency landing. And, we shall not forget, all these geographies coexist in time and space.

2.4.2 The contradiction between plurality and categorization

Acknowledging the plurality of migrant and non-migrant populations implies to question the relation between the way the territory is organized and governed and the irreducible variety of its practices of use. Assuming that plural populations make a set of different uses of the same city, Crosta (2018) argues that our government system does not provide 'political space' to those who actually 'build' the territory through the use they make of it. This relates and reveals a broader crisis of urban policy, which is rooted in the ordinary principle of territorial sovereignty and that also triggers questions around political representation and the incapacity of addressing issues raised by 'unconventional' urban dwellers, as urban populations.[27] Addressing this point, Pasqui (2008) proposes to discuss around the notion of 'politics of populations' where the double genitive stays both for 'for' and 'by' urban populations. He argues that this perspective has at least three consequences for urban policy; in the first place it claims to rethink the relation between political legitimacy, based on territorial sovereignty and the variety of practices that define territories today, this claims for opening to tools of co-planning rather than hierarchical systems. Second, the variety and temporal complexity of urban populations' practices question traditional mechanisms of representation and identification of collective interests. Third, this perspective claims for a renewed attention on the everyday dimension, namely policy that can grasp the complexity of everyday practices – for instance not only addressing wide strategies for public transport but also the quality of trains or waiting spaces in stations (Pasqui, 2017). These are very broad topics that deserve more space than the one provided in this work; however, it is important to hint at them to contextualize the challenge that migrant populations – among others – set. There emerges a need for pluralization as an essential value to be acknowledged in the analysis of populations, uses and territories and to be implemented through urban policy. This challenge applies also in the context of migration journeys and landings. On the one hand, we witness a wide range of profiles, practices and geographies and, on the other hand, categories that narrow this multiplicity into objects of governance – forced-voluntary, economic migrant-asylum seeker etc. – clearly defined by the regulating state (Papadopoulos and Tsianos, 2013; Meeus et al., 2020).

2.4.3 Grounding the challenge of pluralization

The need for pluralization introduces a critique of the strict normativity of planning; this critique is indeed quite recurrent in the debate on arrival processes and spaces. Cremaschi (2016) highlights how the porosity of our cities is very limited, and they are functionally 'dried up'; in other words, cities reject anything that does not fit into given definitions and procedures. More specifically referring to arrival infrastructures and the related place-based activities, Meeus *et al.* (2020) argue that

> apart from a more adjusted, less normative (building) regulatory framework, in many cases these activities would also benefit from the introduction of less strict law policy areas/zones so that the potential for diverse and still unimaginable futuring vectors can be realised.
>
> (*ibidem*, p. 18)

It follows that acknowledging the pluralization of populations, practices and emerging geographies implies rethinking the strict normativity of planning categories that define the conditions of access and usability of our cities and landing spaces. In other words, it implies questioning what the territorial grips and resistances for migrant landings are and how do they work. In a work on Antwerp, Schillebeeckx *et al.* (2019) underline how so-called ethnic shops often play a crucial role in social networked and information exchange among newcomers; however, the opening hours imposed by strict zonings regulation hinder these functions. In this sense, on a practical level, the question is how to rethink regulatory frameworks on their different levels, so that they can host various conditions of possibility, for different populations and uses. On this point, it is worth mentioning the work of Antonio Tosi (2017), who discusses about the access to housing for 'the very poor,' including destitute migrants, refugees and asylum seekers. Within a brilliant reflection on the existing trade-off between quality and access to housing, he suggests that to grasp the socio-spatial complexity of these populations, we should question the conditions of access to housing, no more starting from given categories, but rather from the actual housing practices of these populations and implementing conditions of access and quality across different fields of policies. Against the inadequacy of existing categories and measures in defining the actual practices in use in contemporary cities, what emerges is the need to rethink the condition of access and use of the territory. And this, as many authors suggest, can be done on the one hand, by recognizing the everyday practices of these populations and learning from them and, on the other hand, by working on regulatory frameworks that allow for actual access and use of the territory.

2.5 Insightful experiences

We have unpacked landing into three main dimensions, which point out the main characters of this process and shed light on the main challenges linked to it. Challenges are both those that people on the move experience and those – that interest us in this work – that those who govern and organize cities should engage with. To trigger the latter reflection, we will mention four interesting experiences, as ways of furthering the conceptual issues discussed in this chapter.[28]

2.5.1 The architecture collective HEIM, thinking permanent for the temporary

In a recent paper on arrival infrastructures, Meeus *et al.* (2020) mention the experience of a Belgian architecture collective HEIM, which has worked in the European context on the possibility of building permanent arrival infrastructures for temporary residence in cities (Beeckmans, 2017). In a framework where the answers to the so-called refugee crisis in Europe have mostly consisted of provisional and 'temporary' solutions to the apparent temporary presence of newcomers, HEIM's work on housing typologies heads in the opposite direction. Through design research and inspired by valuable initiatives of civil society organizations in the Netherlands and abroad, the collective investigates how to develop a permanent and flexible structure for temporary housing. Their reflections and projects work on different levels. In the first place, on an urban scale, they underline the need to think of reception, not only through primary needs – the provision of 'bread, beds, and bathrooms,' as they mention – but also through secondary ones. This highlights a range of spaces and functions in the city – shops, public spaces etc. – that can be structurally strengthened both for newcomers and local residents. Second, on a design and architectural level, they work on the concept of permanent and flexible structures. Starting from a critique to the failed temporariness of common reception facilities, which often are provisional and *ad hoc* structures that however easily remain on the long term, the collective proposes to work on more generalist and permanent structures that however include flexible typologies. Indeed, they frame the demand of migrant newcomers within a broader demand for more flexible and new housing typology, which stems from new and changing urban dwellers' profiles. These reflections are mirrored in the project proposal for the renovation of three vacant built areas and two churches in Aalst, to turn into housing for 'people on the move.' The projects pay particular attention to the relationship with the urban context, identifying strategic and shareable places, where also to address the secondary needs of residents. On a design scale, they choose a large target group of 'people on the run,' thus including the needs of migrants within a broader framework of mobile urban dwellers. Still on a design level, they do not only envision a scenario for present housing needs but also work on more and alternative ones, including functions needed by the urban context and Municipality. This effort gives a concrete example of the flexibility they propose as a design principle. Finally, they also mention the relevance of thinking about the sustainability of such projects. In this sense, they mention financial structures, or models to be strengthened – among them shared ownership, social rental offices for the management – and actors to be involved. The experience of the Belgian architecture collective emplaces many of the theoretical questions about temporariness and permanence into the realm of urban and architectural design. Particularly, it represents an interesting effort to work within the binaries of what is temporary and permanent, into more mixed solutions.

2.5.2 The town of Grande-Synthe, ensuring shelters also to whom not willing to stay

Michel Agier, the coordinator of the Babels project, together with a number of co-authors, dedicated a whole volume to the experience of a French town, Grande-Synthe (Agier *et al.*, 2018). Following the way Grande-Synthe interpreted its role as a border town, they define it as a *Ville Accueillente* (Eng. a welcoming city), where to discuss, theoretically and empirically, questions of exile, architecture and the city. In the backlash of the so-called European 'refugees' crisis,' a tent settlement growing at the town's doors reached 5,000 inhabitants; these migrants were mainly people who were trying to cross the border with the United Kingdom and were not willing to stay in France. Their condition reflects very well the notion of 'transmigrants,' as the public debate would name them; namely people whose will was to cross the border and whose arrival in Grande-Synthe was open to further transit. In March 2016, the Mayor decided to intervene; however, not by dismantling the camp but by bettering the condition of the tent settlement that had grown. Light measures and interventions consisted of turning the tents into wooden structures, still not considered as permanent but offering better living conditions to its inhabitants. Initially, the National government had asked to dismantle the camp, arguing that it was unacceptable to allow an 'informal' settlement of that size. Not far from this town, indeed, the town of Calais had already become well known as the 'jungle,' for the features of the camp that was set up and where people would live in dramatic conditions. However, the town administration understood that what at the local level could be defined as an informal settlement also represented a crucial node for the migration trajectory toward the United Kingdom. Making the camp and its inhabitants permanent, or dismantling it, would have prevented that space from functioning as a point of temporary arrival and take off. Thus, the interventions were initially promoted by the municipality and an international NGO, whereas the National government was eventually forced to take part in the initiative. This experience raised a political debate; Valerie Fouche-Dufoix (2018, pp. 296–298) underlines the intense political value of the mayor's move and argues that the choice to 'see' – and acknowledge – the presence of migrants and 'make it visible,' through its temporal nuances, is a strong political act and a project of society. The central government's standpoint clearly embodied an approach where permanence prevails over temporariness as the main principle for obtaining the right to dwell in a certain territory. Here migrants who were not willing to stay were considered somehow 'deportable.' Instead, the Mayor of Grande-Synthe proposed a nuanced approach to the permanent-temporary and sedentary-mobile binaries and moved in the direction of liberating temporariness and acknowledging the right for circular mobilities, by granting a decent dwelling to people on the move. In this sense, this experiment of a temporary settlement with standards and aspirations of permanence, realized through an elastic shape and the flexibility of spaces and individuals represents an insightful experience (Agier *et al.*, 2018).

2.5.3 The Milanese central hub, managing plural trajectories through reception

Between 2015 and 2016, Milan witnessed unprecedented numbers of arrivals; before the stricter control of northern Italian borders, shortly after having arrived, many attempted to depart to reach northern European countries. Within this context, reception facilities 'popped up' throughout the city, where managing third-sector actors had available structures – unused warehouses, barracks, schools and sport centers became first reception facilities. Only one kilometer from the central train station, which was also the main arrival point, the Municipality set up a hub, intended as a 'filter' center. Here, before entering and being registered in the official reception system, people could stop. Many of the hosts meant to keep traveling since when borders became harder to cross, arrivals dropped and the hub turned into a public orientation helpdesk addressing homeless people. Around 2013, at the very beginning of the so-called Syrian crisis, less than 1 percent of migrants arriving in Milan asked for asylum in Italy, they only had a few days to recover and rest. At the time, Milan Central Station's landings were thus highly open to further transit; many migrants not willing to enter the Italian reception system used to wait in the station hall, helped in the same spaces by volunteers and third sector's operators. The local administration realized that the reception system was lacking a 'filter,' which could welcome people arriving but only transiting for a few hours or days. In July 2015, a space previously hosting recreational rooms for railway workers was opened as a reception hub not far from the station's main hall. After ten months this place proved to be too small, and the service moved to a large vacant warehouse a kilometer away from the station. The new space continued playing the role of filter within the reception system, even when the number of transit migrants dramatically decreased; in the following months, the hub was provided with a further space of dorms for those migrants who were willing to ask for asylum in Italy and therefore would have entered the first reception system dimension. This center was managed by a third-sector association, Fondazione Progetto Arca, in collaboration with others that would follow specific activities or initiatives and under the supervision of the Municipality; the warehouses were freely rendered available for temporary use by the National Railway Institution, *Ferrovie dello Stato*. The hub worked for two years as a real filter place, thus ensuring access to all people coming from the near Central Station, requiring only an informal registration – managed by Fondazione Progetto Arca, only for the organization of the activities and services of the hub – this also allowed an easy exit. This experience ended in 2017, when arrivals widely decreased, and the center was closed and converted into a Help Center directly managed by the Municipality and mostly addressing homeless people in Milan.[29] In the same spaces, a light reconfiguration of the layout supported the establishment of this new public service, which developed in continuity with the reception experience. The reasons why this center was opened in fact strongly link to the need to address the condition of 'transmigration,' mentioned by Tarrius (2010) and Meeus *et al.* (2020) and fully represent the mobility paradigm. The role of the hub is grounded on the acknowledgment of Milan as a territory of circulation, different from the logic of reception centers that have very specific access and exit procedures. This experience did not come without tensions nor heavy contradictions; on the one hand, it did provide access to a crucial service for landing migrants, managing to address the openness of their condition. On the other hand, this situation proved unbearable for a public European Municipality: the open access policy of the hub often resulted in an uncontrolled number of people – sometimes also Italians – using the space, in poor conditions. This, together with the decrease of migrants' arrivals and mainly transits in Milan, eventually led to the transformation of this service.

2.5.4 The SAIER, a public service for people on the move

Among cities that in the last decades have proved to be on the frontline on reception issues, Barcelona is certainly one of them. It indeed is involved in numerous city networks,[30] where public operators and civil society organizations get together to discuss how migrations can be dealt with locally. In this framework, the Barcelonian public service for 'people on the move,' the SAIER[31] represents an interesting experience, founded more than a decade ago and still working today. The SAIER (Span. *Servicio de Atención a Inmigrantes, Emigrants y Refugiados*; Eng. Care Service for Immigrants, Emigrants and Refugees) is a service specialized in international mobility, founded in 1989, which manages to grant access and usability beyond the legal categories of refugees, asylum seekers, regular and irregular migrants. Through direct access, it provides information and support about the city, immigration, refugee status, imigrations and voluntary return to all people living in Barcelona. This public service is managed by the Municipality together with a range of social organizations, also specializing in legal support, first reception and translation. It is intended as complementary to public social services, and today it provides access to the national program for refugees. People arriving at the SAIER encounter a first reception desk, and immediately after are entitled to have a first interview, with an orientation aim and with multi-lingual front-line staff; this initial reception is the core of the service, on the overall number of accesses, the majority are about general information and orientation requests. The second appointment instead aims at providing the user with a more specialized answer and is managed by specific services with the help of translators when needed. Although the service is open to all mobile populations living in Barcelona, the SAIER specializes in Third Country nationals with less than two years of staying in Spain, with irregular status and no roots. In an interview, Ramon Sanahuja,[32] former Director of the SAIER, declares that 95 percent of their work is on immigration and asylum seekers; over the total number of users, 29 percent are regular migrants, 26 percent are people whose documents are being processed and 46 percent are migrants irregularly staying in Barcelona. Interestingly, indeed the SAIER offers access to the *Padrón* (Eng. Municipal Registry), which in Barcelona is of local competence and to which all people staying in Barcelona for more than six months are asked to register; this registration allows to access essential public health services, education, libraries and other public facilities. In Sanahuja's words, "I am in the Padrón, immigrants are in the Padrón, irregular immigrants are registered as well." The way it addresses the issue of so-called irregular or undocumented migrants makes the SAIER an interesting example to discuss. That of undocumented migrants is a core topic for local administration across Europe, as it shows the emergence of many projects and networks that try to address it.[33] The experience of undocumented migrants and their condition of precariousness is one of the clearest examples of tension between normative categories and actual subjectivities and practices. Whereas holding regal documents is the very first requirement to access and use city public services, the nature and continuous change of norms 'produce' a huge population of undocumented people. Beyond the limits of the service, which we will not investigate here, the SAIER tries to work on this exact node, providing the conditions of accessibility and usability to any

Landing as an open-ended process 51

person 'on the move' staying in Barcelona. In the first place, the idea of working as a 'hub for human mobility' and thus the fact of being open to all people living in a certain time and in a certain space – in this case, Barcelona – matches the notion of populations. The service indeed does not target refugees nor economic migrants, but 'people on the move,' sharing a temporary stay in the city, no matter how long they will stay and where they aim to go next. Second, the broad and open character of the Padrón allows also undocumented migrants to access basic services and to get registered by the local administration; the centrality of the first reception and orientation desks is also guided by the same principle. In this sense, we might argue that the SAIER is a useful example to discuss about the possibility of acknowledging the irreducible variety of populations and competencies of use of the territory and to rethink the conditions of accessibility and usability of policies, services and spaces.

Notes

1 Particularly, authors criticize the normative upward mobility function of these neighborhoods (Schillebeeckx, Oosterlynck and de Decker, 2019), although some still fully recognize to arrival neighborhood this role (Saunders, 2011).
2 These drivers are differently described by the authors: Saunders and Saedimadani talk about factors that 'make' the arrival city, while Schillebeeckx, Oosterlynck and de Decker rather address them as 'spheres' within which understanding the resourcefulness of arrival neighborhoods.
3 The research work by Florian Günther, Heike Hanhörster, Nils Hans, Jan Polívka, 2019. *Die Produktion von Ankunftsquartieren Zur Rolle des Wohnungsbestands und seiner Dynamiken für die sozialräumliche Segregation*, deepens the question of housing in arrival neighborhoods.
4 Some examples reported in the literature are not only public welfare centers, neighborhood centers, social housing, community health centers and centers to help drug users but also faith-based organizations.
5 For instance, northern African countries after the Arab Spring have been major departure countries; only some years later, they have turned into arrival and transit territories for people coming from central and southern Africa and from Asia (Kassar and Dourgnon, 2014); today, again, northern African countries witness large groups of nationals leaving for Europe (REACH and Mercy Corps, 2018; Migreurop and FTDES, 2020). On the other coast of the Mediterranean, southern European countries in the last five years, following the stricter application of the Dublin Agreement, stopped being transit countries and have experienced a steep increase in

52 *Landing as an open-ended process*

asylum requests. Whereas, on the eastern coasts, after the Syrian crisis, Lebanon and Turkey have found themselves receiving the highest number of Syrian refugees (UNHCR, 2020).

6 The policy perspective is built upon a personal work experience at the European Commission, which she conducted in the same years.
7 The literature on refugee camps addresses the unsolved tension between permanent and temporary that characterizes these settlements (Minca, 2015).
8 Precisely from Blommaert's (2014) work on *Infrastructures of superdiversity: Conviviality and language in Antwerp neighborhood*.
9 Particularly, the work on the politics of arrival by Meeus *et al.* (2019) represents a starting point for the proposed analytical distinction into the three topics of temporality, territoriality and populations and uses.
10 To describe this concept, La Cecla (1993) uses the expression 'individual impermanence and the collective permanence' of migrants.
11 Interestingly, the temporal dimension of migration processes is debated also in other disciplines; for instance, social theory scholars (Cwerner, 2001; Griffiths, Rogers and Anderson, 2013; Grønseth, 2013; Mezzadra and Neilson, 2013) argue that it is a crucial topic to investigate migration as a complex phenomenon – intertwined with other social processes such as globalization and decolonization (Fontanari, 2019).
12 Interestingly, this concept emerges also from Khosravi's work (2010).
13 They write that liberation across these two meetings takes various forms – greater mobility, access to social protection, better working and living conditions, longer term and more sustainable financing of programs for nonprofit agencies as well as less burdensome accountability rules.
14 His chapter is titled *Temporal orders, re-collective justice, and the making of untimely states*.
15 We could add as in the case of temporary residence permits.
16 We could add as for 'irregular migrants.'
17 This work has been exhibited in the 2016 Venice Biennale.
18 For instance, they mention that a flexible temporary governance system is created to act as a surrogate for what might have been more permanent.
19 Some references are Sennett (2006) and Waldheim (2012).
20 The term 'territoriality' is here used in relation to the notion of 'territory,' intended as 'the nexus between practices of use and the material part of the world (houses, streets, squares...)' (Pasqui, 2017). It aims at highlighting the link between spaces and practices of landing, in their reciprocal bond (Gaeta, 2018); namely, always intending territories as inextricably related to their practices of use. In the work, territoriality has a primarily descriptive sense, that however is aware and hints at the broader normative notion of this concept, discussed around the question of social and spatial control in a wide international and national literature (among the others, Sack, 1986; Mazza, 1998; Governa, 2005; Raffestin, 2012). The following

reflections on landing, in theoretical and mainly empirical terms, echo the meaning and forms of territoriality – for instance, the institutional one when discussing the relation between spaces of services, and practices. A development of thoughts in this sense is not the object of this work and could represent an interesting path of future elaboration.

21 Tarrius' works explicitly assume a Western and European perspective, although trying to unpack it 'from within.'
22 This argument was introduced by Bruno Meeus, during a seminar held on January 26, 2021, at Politecnico di Milano and organized by the author.
23 We may question, which languages? The fact that reception services often only include the teaching of local languages is an example of how little the mobility question is considered, as if they were given for granted that arriving migrants will stay.
24 On the role of desires and aspirations, the African writer Clariste Soh Moube (2009) describes how the desires filled with hope for a better future are a necessary tool for migrants who undertake those infinite and dangerous travels across Africa heading to Europe. 'Desires are forces against the immobility and length suspension typical of migrants' lives between borders' and 'having a future perspective, albeit vague and blurred, means having a "condition of possibility" (Butler, 1997) in which the subject acts and moves on despite the subjection in which present life is embedded' (Fontanari, 2019, pp. 193–194).
25 On the term practice, she specifies, 'I use the concept of "practices" to point out the active role of my research protagonists in live within those structural constraints exposed in the previous chapters' (Fontanari, 2019, p. 218).
26 de Certeau (1984) distinguishes between 'strategies' and 'tactics,' the former refers to a structure and can be thought autonomously, instead the latter is intended as a 'calculus which cannot count on a "proper" (spatial or institutional localization) […] The place of a tactic belongs to the other' (de Certau, 1984, xix). Thus, for instance, the 'tactics of survival' are based on complex intersubjective relations of sociality, intimacy, and affect.
27 The work of Tosi (starting from 1994) on welfare provision addresses this topic very clearly and claims the need to overcome the 'administrative theory of needs' to grasp the socio-spatial complexity of old and new urban populations.
28 They shall not be intended as 'good practices' or 'successful case studies,' and the idea is rather to report practical experiences that embody some characteristics of the debate and allow for its problematization.
29 The website of the current service is accessible at this link www.comune.milano.it/servizi/centro-aiuto-stazione-centrale1 (last accessed on May 07, 2021).
30 Barcelona defined itself as a City Refuge, and its municipality has taken part in projects such as Admin4All, organized by the IOM, and in networks

such as C-Mise (City Initiative for Migrants with Irregular Status in Europe). On the two, more information is available at these links https://admin4all.eu/ and www.compas.ox.ac.uk/project/city-initiative-on-irregular-migrants-in-europe-c-mise/ (last accessed on October 10, 2021).
31 Information are available at this link https://ajuntament.barcelona.cat/novaciutadania/es/servicio-de-atencion-inmigrantes-emigrantes-y-refugiados-saier (last accessed on May 17, 2021).
32 Interview with Ramon Sanahuja, held in Barcelona on November 8, 2019, by Benedetta Marani for the research group FAMI CapacityMetro-Italia, coordinated by Prof. Stefania Sabatinelli and Prof. Massimo Bricocoli, Politecnico di Milano.
33 An example is the 'City initiative in migrants with irregular status in EU.'

References

Adam, I. and Caponio, T. (2019) "Research on the multi-level governance of migration and migrant integration: Reversed pyramids," in Weinar, A., Bonjour, S., and Zhyznomirska, L. (eds.) *The Routledge handbook of the politics of migration in Europe*. London and New York: Routledge, p. 466.

Agier, M. et al. (2018) *La ville accueillante: accueillir à Grande-Synthe, questions théoriques et pratiques sur les exilés, l'architecture et la ville*. Lyon: PUCA.

Al-Ali, N., Black, R. and Koser, K. (2001) "The limits to 'transnationalism': Bosnian and Eritrean refugees in Europe as emerging transnational communities," *Ethnic and Racial Studies*, 24(4), pp. 578–600. http://eprints.soas.ac.uk/4868/

Ambrosini, M. (2018) *Irregular immigration in Southern Europe. Actors, dynamics and governance*. Cham: Palgrave Macmillan.

Ambrosini, M. and Fontanari, E. (2018) "Into the interstices: Everyday practices of refugees and their supporters in Europe's migration 'Crisis,'" *Sociology*, 52(3), pp. 587–603. doi: 10.1177/0038038518759458

Bailey, A. J., et al. (2002) "(Re)producing Salvadoran transnational geographies," *Annals of the Association of American Geographers*, 92(1), pp. 125–144. doi: 10.1111/1467-8306.00283

Baldassar, L. (2008) "Missing kin and longing to be together: Emotions and the construction of co-presence in transnational relationships," *Journal of Intercultural Studies*, 29(3), pp. 247–266. doi: 10.1080/07256860802169196

Bauder, H. (2017) "Sanctuary cities: Policies and practices in international perspective," *International Migration*, 55(2), pp. 174–187. doi: 10.1111/imig.12308

Beeckmans, L. (2017) *Wonen in Diversiteit. Inclusieve woonvormen voor nieuwkomers*. Antwerp: HEIM in samenwerking met het Vlaams

Architectuurinstituut, de Singel Internationale Kunstcampus en het Team Vlaams Bouwmeester.
Bernardie-Tahir, N. and Schmoll, C. (2018) *Méditerranée des frontières à la dérive*. Lyon: Le passager clandestin.
Biehl, K. S. (2014) "Exploring migration, diversification and urban transformation in contemporary Istanbul: The case of Kumkapı," *Working papers, Max-Planck-Institut zur Erforschung Multireligiöser und Multiethnischer Gesellschaften* 11,14.
Bishop, P. and Williams, L. (2012) *The temporary city*. 1st ed. Oxon-New York: Routledge. Available at: www.routledge.com/The-Temporary-City/Bishop-Williams/p/book/9780415670562 (last accessed on April 28, 2021).
Black, R. et al. (eds.) (2010) *A continent moving west?: EU enlargement and labour migration from Central and Eastern Europe* (IMISCoe Research). Amsterdam: Amsterdam University Press.
Blommaert, J. (2014) "Infrastructures of superdiversity: Conviviality and language in an Antwerp neighborhood," *European Journal of Cultural Studies*, 17(4), pp. 431–451. doi: 10.1177/1367549413510421
Bontemps, V., Makaremi, C. and Mazouz, S. (2018) *Entre accueil et rejet: ce que les villes font aux migrants*. Lyon: Le passager clandestin.
Bovo, M. (2020) "How the presence of newly arrived migrants challenges urban spaces: Three perspectives from recent literature," *Urban Planning*, 5(3), pp. 23–32. doi: 10.17645/up.v5i3.2894
Brekke, J.-P. and Brochmann, G. (2015) "Stuck in transit: Secondary migration of asylum seekers in Europe, national differences, and the Dublin regulation," *Journal of Refugee Studies*, 28(2), pp. 145–162. doi: 10.1093/jrs/feu028.
Bressan, M. and Tosi Cambini, S. (2011) *Zone di transizione Etnografia urbana nei quartieri e nello spazio pubblico*. Bologna: Il Mulino.
Butler, J. (1997) *The psychic life of power: Theories in subjection*. Stanford, CA: Stanford University Press.
Castells, M. (1989) *The informational city: Information, technologu, Economic restructuring, and the urban regional process*. Oxford: Basil Blackwell.
Cattacin, S. (2006) "Why not 'ghettos'? The governance of migration in the splintering city," Willy Brandt series of working papers in International Migration, Migration and Ethnic Relations 6/2, Malmo University, Sweden.
Collins, F. L. (2012) "Transnational mobilities and urban spatialities," *Progress in Human Geography*, 36(3), pp. 316–335. doi: 10.1177/0309132511423126
Collins, F. L. (2018) "Desire as a theory for migration studies: Temporality, assemblage and becoming in the narratives of migrants," *Journal of Ethnic and Migration Studies*, 44(6), pp. 964–980. doi: 10.1080/1369183X.2017.1384147

Cremaschi, M. (2016) ""Spazi e 'cose' dell'immigrazione," *Quaderni di Urbanistica3 – Inclusione fragile*." Migrazioni nei centri minori del Lazio, 11, pp. 119–125.
Cresswell, T. (2006) *On the move. Mobility in the modern Western World.* New York and London: Routledge.
Crosta, P. L. (2010) *Pratiche. Il territorio "è l'uso che se ne fa."* Milan: FrancoAngeli.
Crosta, P. L. (2018) "Territori," in Bifulco, L., Borghi, V., and Bricocoli, M. (eds.) *Azione pubblica. Un glossario Sui Generis.* Milan: Mimesis, pp. 145–150.
Cwerner, S. B. (2001) "The times of migrations," *Journal of Ethnic and Migration Studies*, 27(1), pp. 7–36. doi: 10.1080/13691830125283
Dahdah, A., Puig, N. and Abou Zaki, H. (2018) *Exils syriens: Parcours et ancrages (Liban, Turquie, Europe)*. Lyon: Le passager clandestin.
Darling, J. (2017) "Forced migration and the city: Irregularity, informality, and the politics of presence," *Progress in Human Geography*, 41(2), pp. 178–198. https://doi.org/10.1177/0309132516629004
de Certau, M. (1984) *The practice of everyday life*. Berkeley, CA: University of California Press.
de Haas, H. (2005) "International migration, remittances and development: Myths and facts," *Third World Quarterly*, 26(8), pp. 1269–1284. doi: 10.1080/01436590500336757
de Haas, H. (2010a) "Migration and development: A theoretical perspective," *International Migration Review*, 44(1), pp. 227–264. doi: 10.1111/j.1747-7379.2009.00804
de Haas, H. (2010b) "The internal dynamics of migration processes. A theoretical inquiry," *Journal of Ethnic and Migration Studies*, 36(10), pp. 1–31. doi: 10.1080/1369183X.2010.489361
Donzelot, J. (2011) "Le chantier de la citoyenneté urbaine," *Esprit (1940–)*, 373(3/4), pp. 118–136. Available at: www.jstor.org/stable/24271073
Faist, T. (2000) *The volume and dynamics of international migration and transnational social spaces*. Oxford: Clarendon-Oxford University Press.
Faist, T. (2013) "No the mobility turn: A new paradigm for the social sciences?," *Ethnic and Racial Studies*, 36(11), pp. 1637–1646. doi: 10.1080/01419870.2013.812229
Fernandez, L. and Olson, J. (2011) "No to live, love and work anywhere you please: Critical exchange on Arizona and the struggle for locomotion," *Contemporary Political Theory*, 10, pp. 415–417.
Fontanari, E. (2019) *Lives in transit: An ethnographic study of refugees' subjectivity across European borders*. London: Routledge.
Foucher-Dufoix, V. (2018) "De la ville refuge à la ville accueillante. Figure de l'elu hospitalier," in Agier, M. et al. (eds.) *La ville accueillante. Accueillir a Grande-Synthe, questions théoriques et pratiques sur les exilés, l'architecture et la ville*. Lyon: PUCA, pp. 243–300.

Gaeta, L. (2018) *La civiltà dei confini. Pratiche quotidiane e forme di cittadinanza*. Rome: Carocci.

Gardesse, C. and Lelévrier, C. (2020) "Refugees and asylum seekers dispersed in non-metropolitan French cities: Do housing opportunities mean housing access?," *Urban Planning*, 5(3), pp. 138–149. doi: 10.17645/up.v5i3.2926

Glick Schiller, N., Basch, L. and Blanc-Szanton, C. (1995) "From immigrant to transmigrant: Theorizing transational migration," *Anthropology Quarterly*, 68(1), pp. 48–63. doi: 10.2307/3317464

Glick Schiller, N. and Salazar, N. B. (2013) "Regimes of mobility across the globe," *Journal of Ethnic and Migration Studies*, 39(2), pp. 183–200. doi: 10.1080/1369183X.2013.723253

Glick Schiller, N. and Wimmer, A. (2002) "Methodological nationalism and beyond: Nation-state building, migration and the social sciences," *Global Networks*, 2(4), pp. 301–334. doi: 10.1111/1471-0374.00043

Global Commission on International Migration (GCIM) (2005) *Migration in an interconnected world: New directions for action*. Report of the Global Commission on International Migration. Geneva.

Governa, F. (2005) "Sul ruolo attivo della territorialità," in Dematteis, G. and Governa, F. (eds.) *Territorialità. sviluppo locale, sostenibilità. Il modello SLoT*. Milan: FrancoAngeli.

Griffiths, M. (2014) "Out of time: The temporal uncertainties of refused asylum seekers and immigration detainees," *Journal of Ethnic and Migration Studies*, 40 (12), pp. 1991–2009. doi: 10.1080/1369183X.2014.907737

Griffiths, M., Rogers, A. and Anderson, B. (2013) Migration, time and temporalities: review and prospect. COMPAS Research Resources Paper, March 2013. Available at: www.compas.ox.ac.uk/wp-content/uploads/RR-2013-Migration_Time_Temporalities.pdf (last accessed on December 26, 2023).

Grønseth, A. S. (eds.). (2013) *Being human, being migrant: Senses of self and well-being*. New York: Berghahn Books, pp. 1–26. doi: doi.org/10.3167/9781782380450

Günther, F. et al. (2019) Die Produktion von Ankunftsquartieren Zur Rolle des Wohnungsbestands und seiner Dynamiken für die sozialräumliche Segregation FGW-Studie Integrierende Stadtentwicklung 17.

Hanhörster, H. and Wessendorf, S. (2020) "The role of arrival areas for migrant integration and resource access," *Urban Planning*, 5(3), pp. 1–10. doi: 10.17645/up.v5i3.2891

Hannam, K., Sheller, M. and Urry, J. (2006) "Editorial: Mobilities, immobilities and moorings," *Mobilities*, 1(1), pp. 1–22. doi: 10.1080/17450100500489189

Hans, N. et al. (2019) "Die Rolle von Ankunftsräumen für die Integration Zugewanderter. Eine kritische Diskussion des Forschungsstandes," *Raumforschung und Raumordnung*, 77(5), pp. 122–135. doi: 10.2478/rara-2019-0019

Huang, S. and Yeoh, B. S. A. (2007) "Emotional labour and transnational domestic work: The moving geographies of 'Maid Abuse' in Singapore," *Mobilities*, 2(2), pp. 195–217. doi: 10.1080/17450100701381557

Isin, E. F. and Rygiel, K. (2007) "Abject spaces: Frontiers, zones, camps," in Dauphinee, E. and Masters, C. (eds.) *The logics of biopower and the war on terror*. Palgrave Macmillan US, pp. 181–203. doi: 10.1007/978-1-137-04379-5_9

Kassar, H. and Dourgnon, P. (2014) "The big crossing: Illegal boat migrants in the Mediterranean," *European Journal of Public Health*, 24(1), pp. 11–15.

Keil, R. (2017) *Suburban planet: Making the world urban from the outside*. Hoboken, NJ: John Wiley.

Khosravi, S. (2010) *"Illegal" traveller, An auto-ethnography of borders*. London: Palgrave Macmillan.

Kristeva, J. (1982) *Powers of horror: An essay on abjection*. New York: Columbia University Press.

La Cecla, F. (1993) *Mente locale. Per un'antropologia dell'abitare*. Milan: Elèuthera.

Latham, R. (2014) "Temporal orders, re-collective justice, and the making of untimely states," in Vosko, L. F., Preston, V., and Latham, R. (eds.) *Liberating temporariness?: Migration, work, and citizenship in an age of insecurity*. Kingston, Ontario: McGill-Queen's Univeristy Press, pp. 272–295.

Lenard, P. T. and Straehle, C. (2012) *Legislated Iinequality: Temporary labour migration in Canada*. Kingston, Ontario: McGill-Queen's Univeristy Press.

Levitt, P. and Glick Schiller, N. (2004) "Conceptualizing simultaneity: A transnational social field perspective on society," *International Migration Review*, 38(3), pp. 1002–1039.

Malecki, E. J. and Ewers, M. C. (2007) "Labor migration to world cities: With a research agenda for the Arab Gulf," *Progress in Human Geography*, 31(4), pp. 467–484. doi: 10.1177/0309132507079501

Malkki, L. (1992) "National geographic: The rooting of peoples and the territorialization of national identity among scholars and refugees," *Cultural Anthropology*, 7(1), pp. 24–44. doi: 10.1525/can.1992.7.1.02a00030

Martinotti, G. (1993) *Metropoli. La nuova morfologia sociale della città*. Bologna: Il Mulino.

Mazza, L. (1998) *Appunti di urbanistica 1998/1999*. Facoltà di Architettura, Campus Leonardo, Politecnico di Milano.

Meeus, B. et al. (2020) "Broadening the urban planning repertoire with an 'Arrival Infrastructures' perspective," *Urban Planning*, 5(3), pp. 11–22. doi: 10.17645/up.v5i3.3116

Meeus, B., Arnaut, K. and van Heur, B. (2019) *Arrival infrastructures: Migration and urban social mobilities, arrival infrastructures: Migration and urban social mobilities*. Springer International Publishing. doi: 10.1007/978-3-319-91167-0

Mehrotra, R. and Vera, F. (2015) *Mapping the ephemeral megacity*. Berlin: Harvard South Asia Institute, Hatje Cantz Verlag.
Mehrotra, R., Vera, F. and Mayoral, J. (2017) *Ephemeral urbanism. Does permanence matter?* Trento: ListLab.
Mezzadra, S. (2015) "The proliferation of borders and the right to escape," in Jansen, Y., Celikates, R., and de Bloois, J. (eds.) *The irregularization of migration in contemporary Europe: Detention, deportation, drowning*. London/New York: Rowman & Littlefield, pp. 121–135.
Mezzadra, S. and Neilson, B. (2013) *Border as method, or the multiplication of labor*. Durham, NC and London: Duke University Press.
Migreurop and FTDES (2020) *Politiques du non-accueil en Tunisie. Des acteurs humanitaires au service des politiques sécuritaires européennes*. www.gisti.org/IMG/pdf/hc_2020_migreurop-ftdes_rapport-tunisie.pdf (last accessed on March 11, 2024).
Minca, C. (2015) "Geographies of the camp," *Political Geography*, 49, pp. 74–83.
Papadopoulos, D. and Tsianos, V. (2013) "After citizenship: Autonomy of migration, organisational ontology and mobile commons," *Citizenship Studies*, 17(2), pp. 178–196. doi: 10.1080/13621025.2013.780736
Papadopoulou-Kourkoula, A. (2008) *Transit migration: The missing link between emigration and settlement*. New York: Palgrave Macmillan.
Papastergiadis, N. (2000) *The turbulence of migration. Globalization deterritorialization and hybridity*. Cambridge: Polity Press.
Park, R. E., Burgess, E. and McKenzie, R. D. (1925) *The city*. Chicago, IL: University of Chicago Press.
Pasqui, G. (2008) *Città, popolazioni e politiche*. Milan: Jaka Book.
Pasqui, G. (2017) *Urbanistica oggi*. Piccolo lessico critico. Rome: Donzelli Editore.
Pezzoni, N. (2013) *La città sradicata. Geografie dell'abitare contemporaneo. I migranti mappano Milano*. Milan: O barra O edizioni.
Portes, A., Guarnizo, L. E. and Landolt, P. (1999) "The study of transnationalism: Pitfalls and promise of an emergent research field," *Ethnic and Racial Studies*, 22(2), pp. 217–237. doi: 10.1080/014198799329468
Raffestin, C. (2012) "Space, territory, and territoriality," *Environment and Planning D: Society and Space*, 30, pp. 121–141. doi: 0.1068/d21311
REACH and Mercy Corps (2018) *Tunisia, country of emigration and return. Migration dynamics since 2011*. Geneva.
Sack, R. D. (1986) *Human territoriality. Its theory and history*. Cambridge: Cambridge University Press.
Saeidimadani, M. (2012) *Arrival space. Der schmale Grat zwischen Erfolg und Scheitern migrantisch geprägter Räume*. Milan (IT), and HCU Hamburg, Hamburg (DE): Politecnico di Milano.
Saunders, D. (2011) *Arrival city: How the largest migration in history is reshaping our world*. London: Windmill Books.

Schapendonk, J. (2012) "Turbulent trajectories: African migrants on their way to the European Union," *Societies*, 2(2), pp. 27–41. doi: 10.3390/soc2020027

Schillebeeckx, E., Oosterlynck, S. and de Decker, P. (2019) "Migration and the resourceful neighborhood: Exploring localized resources in urban zones of transition," in *Arrival infrastructures: Migration and urban social mobilities*. Springer International Publishing, pp. 131–152. doi: 10.1007/978-3-319-91167-0_6

Schiller, N. G., Basch, L. and Blanc-Szanton, C. (1992) "Transnationalism: A new analytic framework for understanding migration," *Annals of the New York Academy of Sciences*, 645, pp. 1–24. doi: 10.1111/j.1749-6632.1992.tb33484.x

Schiller, N. G. and Çağlar, A. (2010) *Locating migration. Rescaling cities and migrants*. Edited by N. Glick Schiller and A. Çağlar. Ithaca, NY): Cornell University Press.

Schmal, P., et al. (2016) *Making Heimat: Germany, arrival country*. Ostfildern (GE): Hatje Cantz Verlag.

Schuermans, N., Schrooten, M. and De Backer, M. L. (2019) "Informele En Formele Sociaalwerkpraktijken Als Aankomstinfrastructuren Voor Nieuwkomers," in Schrooten, M., Thys, R., and Debruyne, P. (eds.) *Sociaal Schaduwwerk: Over Informele Spelers in Het Welzijnslandschap*. Brussels: Politeia, pp. 147–158.

Sennett, R. (2006) "The open city," *LSE Cities*, November. http://downloads.lsecities.net/0_downloads/Berlin_Richard_Sennett_2006-The_Open_City.pdf (last accessed on March 11, 2024).

Simone, A. M. (2004) "People as infrastructure: Intersecting fragments in Johannesburg," *Public Culture*. Duke University Press, pp. 407–429. doi: 10.1215/08992363-16-3-407

Smith, M. P. (2005) "Transnational urbanism revisited," *Journal of Ethnic and Migration Studies*, 31, pp. 235–244. doi: 10.1080/1369183042000339909

Soh Moubé, C. (2009) *La trappola*. Rome: Infinito Edizioni.

Spada, G. and Valentino, N. (2018) *La porta del mare. Socioanalisi narrativa dei dispositivi di gestione neocoloniale dei migranti*. Edited by G. Spada and N. Valentino. Rome: Sensibili alle foglie.

Tarrius, A. (1993) "Territoires circulatoires et espaces urbains: Différentiation des groupes migrants," *Les Annales de la recherche urbaine,*, N°59–60, pp. 51–60.

Tarrius, A. (2010) "Territoires circulatoires et étapes urbaines des transmigrant(e)s," *Regards croisés sur l'economie*, 8(2), pp. 63–70. Available at: www.cairn.info/revue-regards-croises-sur-l-economie-2010-2-page-63.htm (last accessed on December 26, 2023).

Tosi, A. (1994) *Abitanti. Le nuove strategie dell'azione abitativa*. Bologna: Il Mulino.

Tosi, A. (2017) *Le case dei poveri. È ancora possibile pensare un welfare abitativo?* Milan: Mimesis Edizioni.

Tzaninis, Y. (2019) "Cosmopolitanism beyond the city: Discourses and experiences of young migrants in post- suburban Netherlands," *Urban Geography*, 41(1), pp. 143–161. doi:10.1080/02723638.2019.1637212

UNHCR (2020) Global trends. Forced displacement in 2019. Geneva.

Urry, J. (2000) *Sociology beyond societies: Mobilities for the 21st Century.* London: Routledge.

Vertovec, S. (2007) "Super-diversity and its implications," *Ethnic and Racial Studies*, 30(6), pp. 1024–1054. doi: 10.1080/01419870701599465

Vertovec, S. (2015a) "Introduction: Migration, cities, diversities 'Old' and 'New,'" in *Diversities old and new.* London: Palgrave Macmillan UK, pp. 1–20. doi: 10.1057/9781137495488_1

Vertovec, S. (2015b) *Routledge international handbook of diversities studies.* London and New York: Routledge.

Vosko, L. F., Preston, V. and Latham, R. (2014) *Liberating temporariness?: migration, work, and citizenship in an age of insecurity.* Kingston, Ontario: McGill-Queen's University Press.

Waldheim, C. (2012) *The landscape urbanism reader.* Edited by C. Waldheim. San Francisco, CA: Chronicle books.

Werlen, B. (1993) *Society action and space: an alternative human geography.* New York: Routledge.

Wilson, K. L. and Martin, W. A. (1982) "Ethnic enclaves: A comparison of the Cuban and Black economies in Miami," *American Journal of Sociology*, 88(1), pp. 135–160. doi: 10.1007/s13524-011-0058-8

Zigon, J. (2015). "What is a situation? An assemblic ethnography of the drug war." *Cultural Anthropology*, *30*(3), 501–524. doi: 10.14506/ca30.3.07

3 Palermo as crossroads in the central Mediterranean route

It is now time to ground the outlined framework; we will do this along the central Mediterranean route, focusing on the city of Palermo in southern Italy. Interestingly, the lens of landing here will prove particularly useful to address arrival processes as they deploy in this context. In fact, in the Mediterranean case, the nature of migratory movements and how they are regulated strongly impact how arrival develops and spatializes. Much of its open-endedness is directly linked to polycentric interventions of reception, regulation and repression by institutional and non-institutional actors across the Mediterranean and in Europe and to the local politics, policy and practices through which landings have been channeled. More than elsewhere, in this context, assuming an open-ended understanding of arrival, i.e. the landing framework, will be necessary.

3.1 The development of the central route

The Mediterranean Sea has been for many years the central site of economic, political and cultural exchanges, but also that of hegemonic struggles; it has represented a 'vital crossroad' and a 'system of circulation,' so as a barrier and border (Fontanari, 2019). Despite it has now lost part of its ancient centrality, the Mediterranean remains the crossroads of a complex mobility net, where migration processes play a crucial role. In the last two decades, indeed, the 'middle sea' has renewed its role as an area of contested mobilities. In particular, the Mediterranean has become one of the access-ways for migrants trying to reach Europe, "a *battleground* where migrants trace new routes [..]"(Fontanari, 2019, p. 33). Since 2011, the 'Arab Spring' and the

Libyan war marked a turning point in international migration across Africa and Europe, opening later the 'long summer of migration' in 2015 (Hess and Kasparek, 2017). On the other hand, the reaction of European states, who have built a progressively emergency regime to manage the turbulent arrivals of migrants from southern countries. Thus, until today, migrant trajectories bond together what stays before, in between and after the Mediterranean passage from south to north. "The trajectories across these places shed light on what Braudel tries to say about the 'intimate relationship' between the two faces of the Mediterranean" (Fontanari, 2019, p. 34).

Braudel's image of the Mediterranean as a mosaic reminds us that "the fractures and routes across the 'middle sea' are products of history, namely of power reactions and struggles that make the geographic map of the Mediterranean a *political* map" (Fontanari, 2019, p. 34). As Gabriele del Grande (2023) underlines, there are political choices, laws and mechanisms that have defined borders and the ways it was possible to cross them. Within the central Mediterranean route, European migration policies played a core role and intertwine with the autonomous movements of migrants, smuggling and trafficking networks (Fontanari, 2019). In fact, before the 1990s, there were alternative ways of traveling to Europe, from Africa as from the rest of the world: with a passport and a visa. Between the 1980s and 1990s, however, mobility became central in the European project. While progressively opening internal borders for goods, capital and European citizens in the Schengen area, the European Union (EU) started closing and controlling external borders for non-European citizens[1] (Fontanari, 2019, p. 22), and particularly for many Africans. Control mechanisms indeed started operating a choice among those who could freely access the Union, those who needed a visa for temporary or long-term staying and those who needed one even just for transiting by. These measures had a great impact on the development of migratory routes across the sea. Traditionally, immigration has never passed through Lampedusa, Pantelleria, Evros, Cadiz or Ceuta (del Grande, 2023). In the face of the closure of legal ways to reach Europe, the movement demand found an answer in smuggling and trafficking[2] networks, which developed between Africa and Europe. In this sense, Gabriele del Grande (2023) argues that disembarkations are not the causes of immigration policies, but the consequences of visa policies. In a world where mobility is not an exception, this narrative explains how things develop on a broader framework: it shows that alternatives would be possible, and it implies

64 *Palermo as crossroads in the central Mediterranean route*

a strong critique to the Europe Union border regime, described by Mezzadra (2004) as a hybrid regime of variable sovereignty.

Within this framework, policies and the connected bordering practices shape migratory routes, in a continuous opening and closing of different paths (Figure 3.1). Already in the 1990s, routes

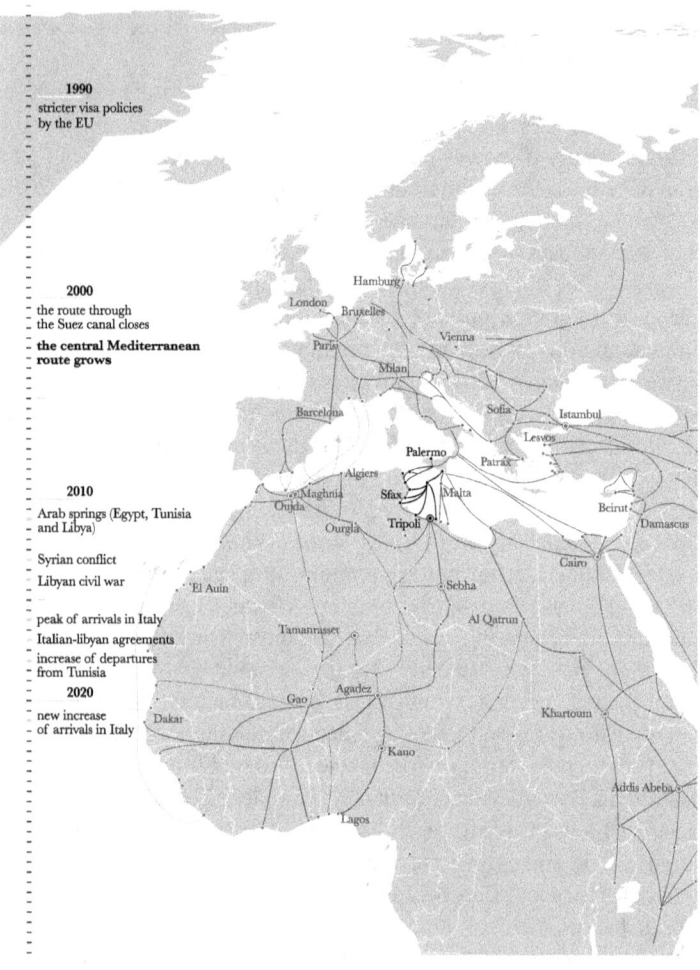

Figure 3.1 The central Mediterranean route and timeline. Elaboration by the author from existing data and maps, 2021.

and ways of reaching Europe started changing and member states' reactions developed through restrictive practices of border enforcement at sea and confinement of people in closed structures.[3] At the beginning of the 2000s, the route through the Suez Canal closed and it increased the centrality of the Sahara Desert. Particularly, it started a process of re-orientation of mixed migration flows[4] by sea, and of smuggling activities to a new geographical area, namely Libya. This country became the main transit area toward Europe while being also one of the major immigration countries in Africa; in the early 2000s, emerged the central Mediterranean migratory route from Libya to the Strait of Sicily. This new route has to be interpreted as result of a combination of historical relationships between Libya and the Sahelian countries, of changes in the Mediterranean routes utilized by human smugglers and in the European policies of controlling them and of the deterioration of the crisis in Sudan and in the Horn of Africa (Ciabarri, 2015). In 2011, a series of uprisings, known as 'Arab Spring,' involved northern African countries; despite being heterogenous, these protests were generally fueled by the widespread economic crisis, the lack of individual freedom and recurrent violations of human rights, which led people – mostly young – to protest. In January 2011, the first uprisings lead to the resignation of the Egyptian President, Hosni Mubarak, and to the fall of the Tunisian regime of Ben Ali. In February 2011, began the insurrection in Libya, which turned into a civil war and witnessed also international military interventions until the end of the war was declared in October 2011, with the death of Gaddafi killed by the rebels. These movements have played a crucial role in the reconfiguration of the fragile geopolitical balance between northern African countries and Europe, and of political relations within Africa. Migratory trajectories have immediately been affected by these facts: cross movements through the Maghreb increased, together with travels toward Europe. From 2011, people from the sub-Saharan regions living in Libya started escaping; most movements were directed toward bordering African countries – over the 790,000 people fleeing from Libya, whereas only 30,000 moved toward Europe (Fontanari, 2019, pp. 40–41, on International Organization for Migration [IOM] data dating 2012). In 2013, the outbreak of the Syrian conflict gave birth to a renovated phase of migration processes in the central Mediterranean area; in 2014, while the number of crossings from Turkey and from Egypt toward Italian coasts started increasing, the Libyan route grew disproportionally. People would reach the northern African country from West Africa, through Agadez in Niger, and from the well-established route from Sudan, fed by departures from refugee camps in Ethiopia and Sudan and partially used also by Syrian. In 2014, the outburst of civil war in Libya set the preconditions for the re-emergence of a complex system of alternative irregular migration routes. In 2015, the increasingly dangerous route from Libya was mainly used by West African nationals, while the route to Greece was most used by Syrians and increasingly also by Eritreans, Afghans, Iraqis, and also African nationals and started expanding fast (Monzini, Nourhan and Pastore, 2015). In the central Mediterranean starting from 2016, the number of sea arrivals in Italy increased of 18 percent – reaching 181,436 arrivals – and registered an unprecedented peak. Already from 2017, and then in 2018, the central Mediterranean route experienced the biggest drop; in 2018 only 23,370 sea arrivals were registered in Italy. The central Mediterranean route today stretches from Libya and Tunisia to Italy (*see* Figure 3.1); whereas the first represents a case on its own, hard to generalize, we will have a closer look into Tunisia and Italy to further understand how migratory trajectories and landings deploy.

3.1.1 Tunisia as one of the last African stopovers

In Tunisia, immigration has not been a field of extensive public policy-making over most of the XX century (Natter, 2019), despite the early reforms of immigration regulations after independence and bilateral international agreements. It has generally followed two directions: on the one hand, a welcoming discourse aiming at attracting competences and investments toward a selected number of foreigners. On the other hand, a generalized securitization of – irregular – migration. In terms of emigration, within a relation with Europe that dates back to World War II and since 1990s and the beginning of the season of the so-called irregular migration, Tunisia has pursued a dual emigration policy: encouraging *and* monitoring Tunisian emigration (Natter, 2019). Today in the country, clear-cut definitions on arrival, departure – and return – experiences and spaces do not make much sense. Instead, all these dimensions overlap in time and space, intertwine with the structural problems of the country, within a contingent and unclear migration policies framework.

Immigration mainly involves sub-Saharan Africans reaching the country; among them, those who can access the country with a visa and overstay it, while many others reach the country by land and ask for asylum. Despite the number of asylum requests with United Nations High Commissioner for Refugees (UNHCR) has increased significantly – from 1,200 in 2018 to 3,746 in January 2020 – the procedure keeps being managed by UNHCR and not by the Tunisian authorities, which often stands against international organizations' actions. The recognition of the refugee status has almost no value in the everyday life of people; migrants, even when holding the UNHCR card, cannot access services, education, legal and health assistance; they cannot work with a regular job contract (Borderline Sicilia, 2019). After crossing the border, migrants concentrate in the camps managed by the International Organization for Migration (IOM) and UNHCR, and to a lesser extent in the urban peripheries. The southeastern region, at the border with Libya, witnesses arrivals of sub-Saharan Africans, who mainly arrive from the neighboring country. Along the border, camps have grown and are managed by international organizations and hardly tolerated by local authorities; depending on the opening and closing of these camps, people also move to close border towns, like Ben Guerdane (Grillo, 2016). After arrival, people who are under the protection of UNHCR or IOM should be provided with accommodation, food and medical care. According to a report of Migreurop and FTDES (2020), UNHCR manages in partnership with the Tunisian Council for Refugees (CTR) three reception centers in southern Tunisia – two in Zarzis, the Zitoun and the Ben Guerdane road center, and one in Medenine the Ibn Khaldoun center. The IOM manages other three in partnership with the Red Cross – in Zarzis, in Medenine and in Megrine for so-called voluntary returns, near Tunis airport. In all cases, the reported conditions are very worrying. Additionally, the UNHCR and the CTR rent apartments or hotels – mainly in Tunis – for refugees and asylum seekers with a good chance to obtain international protection. Discouraged by the inadequacy of the protection granted to them, by the slowness of the various procedures and by the lack of prospects for the future, more and more migrants who have come to Tunisia in search of protection end up returning to Libya, even though they are aware of the risks incurred in this failed and war-torn country (Migreurop and FTDES, 2020).

When landings develop into further projects of departure, the trajectories of sub-Saharan migrants mix, along Tunisian coasts, with the increasing number of Tunisian citizens who take the same path and who have represented in the last years the main nationality of arrivals in Italy. Since 2017, there has been an increase in departures involving Tunisian citizens, the so-called *harraga*.[5] Among the causes of their departure, in addition to structural socio-economic causes, recently there are also psycho-social factors – and the will of social redemption – that fuel a shared desire to escape between young Tunisians (Baroni, 2019). Emigrants are often unemployed young men, between 20 and 24 years old, with an elementary school diploma; many of them have tried unsuccessfully to obtain a visa for Europe (REACH and Mercy Corps, 2018). Mounib Baccari[6] argues that

> to explain this phenomenon, we should refer to poverty, the lack of development in certain disadvantaged regions and youth unemployment, which in the south reaches peaks of 43 per cent. In this sense, the so-called Arab Spring has failed, and the young people who are now leaving from the coasts of Sfax, Monastir, El Haouaria, Zarzis and North of Bizert, are well aware of this, seeking a future elsewhere.
>
> (Paluzzi, 2017)

The *harga* starts with a long incubation of the migration project, which takes place in the most marginalized neighborhoods of large cities – Ettadhamen, Ezzouhour, Douar Hicher, Hammam Lif in the suburbs of Tunis – and in small villages of Tunisia – such as Sidi Bouzid, Redeyef, Ben Gardane, Ras Ajdir, Kasserine (Baroni, 2019). In these areas the word-of-mouth spreads in coffee shops, in public spaces and through the social networks. Social networks also play a crucial role in this sense. The main departure points since 2017 are Mahadia, Sfax, Melita Island and Zarzis; in the last years, these departures have been organized with fishing boats, differently from what happens in Libya. Indeed, the sea arrivals in Italy have been defined 'ghost disembarkation,' since they are less visible than the large boats and numbers arriving from Libya.

Finally, in addition to these mixed movements, the REACH Report (2018) describes a third relevant phenomenon, that of returns – on which data are really scarce. Tunisians going back to their country are mainly forced returnees; however, a small percentage also do it on individual initiative, and to a lesser extent through assisted voluntary return procedures. Upon return, migrants often have to face challenges linked to their socio-economic situation back in Tunisia and to feelings of failure or discomfort; many also report intending to re-emigrate in the future (REACH and Mercy Corps, 2018).

Italy as a southern European gateway

On the other coast of the Mediterranean, the EU increasingly represents a major destination area and, as we have mentioned, its policies have played a major role in shaping migratory trajectories along this route.[7] Among other European countries, Italy has one of the youngest immigration histories; however, in the last decades of the XX century, it rapidly started witnessing immigration flows, which today represent a structural element of its population (Ferrario, 2014, p. 395). Immigration policies have never come into a coherent vision. Instead, they have always had a contingent character changing depending on ongoing events and following political interests, as it shows the use of regularizations (Ita. *sanatoria*)[8] as a constant tool of these policies. The outbreak of the Syrian and Libyan conflicts resulted in a new increase of asylum requests, which steeply grew between 2011 and 2016: while in 2011, only 11.8 percent of extra-EU citizens entered Italy for political asylum or humanitarian protection, in 2016 they represented the 34.3 percent (Colucci, 2018). In the country, asylum requests passed from 17,352 in 2012 to more than 130,000 in 2017 (Frontiere, 2018). Since then, apart from familiar and study reasons, the only legal way to enter Italy remains the asylum request. Thus, asylum has turned into a central question in immigration policies and the main tool of inflows' control.[9]

In the framework of international and European legislations, Italy has developed a reception process in three main steps, to which is related a legal status and specific reception facilities and activities.[10] The first phase is that of rescue, first assistance and identification. Foreign nationals rescued at sea or 'irregularly' entering the national territory are taken to governmental centers, located near the areas of disembarkation or main entry into the country, the so-called hotspots. Other kinds of facilities are the Centers of Permanence for Repatriation (Ita. *Centri di Permanenza per i Rimpatri*) (CPR) where so-called economic migrants who are not recognized the right of asking for asylum are moved, when not left on the territory in condition of irregular stay (Openpolis, 2021). Secondly, the Italian system includes a phase of first reception. Those who express the desire to seek asylum in Italy and are not coming from a safe country are transferred to the Centers of First Reception (Ita. *Centri di Prima Accoglienza/ Centri di Accoglienza per Richiedenti Asilo*) (CPA/CARA), first level reception facilities, where they remain for the time necessary to complete the identification operations – if not previously carried out – and the start of the procedure for the examination of the asylum request. Thirdly, there is a second reception phase: this step develops into the System of Reception and Integration (Ita. *Sistema Accoglienza Integrazione*) (SAI),[11] meant as a gradual accompanying to autonomy and integration. Unlike the first reception, managed centrally, the SAI is coordinated by a national Central Service, whose management is assigned by the Ministry of Interior to the National Association of Italian Municipalities (Ita. *Associazione Nazionale Comuni Italiani*) (ANCI). In 2015 (D.Lgs. 142/2015), during the so-called refugee crisis, the Italian government implemented an extra-ordinary channel of reception and Extraordinary Reception Centers (Ita. *Centri di Accoglienza Straordinaria*) (CAS). Despite this was thought as an exceptional and emergency alternative, it became the major solution to reception; CAS today hosts more than half of asylum seekers hosted in first and second reception facilities. The system establishes that asylum seekers holding a temporary staying permit – obtained already in the first reception phase – can subscribe to the national healthcare system for the length of their permit – six months, before renovation. In the first two months of reception, asylum seekers are not allowed to work; later, only through a regular staying permit they are able to sign a job contract, so as a rent contract. Undocumented migrants have the right to receive essential and urgent health assistance, through a temporary card, and cannot sign job-, or rent contract. In the last years, the frequent changes of government in Italy and the close link between reception policies and public debate have led to numerous changes in the described system, particularly starting from 2018, with the Ministry of Interior Salvini.

Beyond this theoretical division into phases and centers, people experience in most cases do not follow the mentioned steps. By the end of 2017, the Italian reception system reached a little more than 180,000 places,[12] and in 2018 a report by Medici Senza Frontiere (2018) reported at least 10,000 people who were excluded by the reception system between asylum seekers and international or humanitarian protection holders.[13] Thus, beyond the theoretical structure of reception, landings in Italy follow three main paths. Firstly, some migrants, after having arrived on Italian borders, never enter the reception system but directly move to northern European countries or reach rural agricultural areas looking for a job. The first option was very common before 2015, when asylum requests in Italy were low, and despite the Dublin Regulation, Italy used to 'close an eye' and let unregistered migrants transit through the country, and ask for asylum somewhere else in Europe. Today, this path is much more difficult due to stricter border and internal controls; however, migrants with low chances of obtaining protection in Italy – as Maghrebi, whose nation of origin is considered 'safe' – tend to attempt the way north. On the other hand, irregular and exploited work, especially in agriculture, is very widespread in Italy (Corrado and Colloca, 2013). Since jobs are not regularized and there are no formal contracts, migrants are not required to own regular documents and often end up in very precarious and dangerous situations. Secondly, there is the case of those who do enter the reception system but also leave it for various reason – they get expelled or choose to leave. Out of the reception system, migrants enter the realm of undocumented and unregistered life; in this case, time limitations of staying permits and continuous changes in the legislation have had drastic effects on people lives.[14] Indeed, many are stuck into a circular and endless entrance and exit from regularity, between the expirations and renewal of their staying permit or linked to the changing requirements for reception.[15] Thirdly, a percentage of people do manage to get through the whole process of reception and to obtain international protection and in some cases to benefit from it. In this case, however, many of the mentioned issues are only postponed and integration and autonomous access to ordinary services still represent a hard step.[16]

3.2 Palermo, a 'sponge city' and a 'base point'

Palermo, the fifth largest Italian city with 670,000 inhabitants, is the main town and administrative center of Sicily, located on its northwestern coast, facing the Tyrrhenian Sea. To understand Palermo, we cannot forget questions of marginality and isolation, that produced social, economic and political issues (Picone and Schilleci, 2019); as well as the historical presence – and the fight against – Mafia organizations. Demographically, it has undergone the effects of a gradual depopulation and an increase of foreign residents, without reaching however the rates of other Italian cities – in Palermo foreign residents are less than 4 percent of the total population, whereas in Milan they overcome 18 percent (Picone and Schilleci, 2019). Interestingly, since 2011, the city has registered a relatively high number of young residents, in working age, who are defined as sources of a 'potential energy' for the city (Picone and Schilleci, 2019, p. 181). Poverty and unemployment[17] emplace Sicily between the poorest Italian regions; in Palermo, this couples with a structural scarcity of welfare and housing resources, as proves – among others – the fact that the city is the third in Italy for number of homeless people. In the face of the structural scarcity of resources and the lack of public policies for more vulnerable populations, auto-organized and managed practices, in diverse fields, have established 'despite' the administration (Cellamare, 2011; Giampino, Lo Piccolo and Todaro, 2019).

It is within this context that immigration patterns shall be framed, since the 1980s when they started more evidently being bonded to the city development. Interestingly, on this point, many underline the 'porosity' of Palermo, 'a sponge city' as Alessandro Dal Lago describes it,[18] that among other southern Italian cities (Cremaschi and Lieto, 2020), has allowed for different kinds of placement and arrangements between local populations and newcomers. Many agree that immigration processes have rarely produced evident social tension (Leone, 2013), although they do embody clear contradictions. Palermo today – more than a destination – is an entry point to Italy and Europe, as it shows the relatively low rate of foreign residents with respect to the number of arrivals (Leone, 2013; Greco and Tumminelli, 2020). Starting 2014-2015, as in the rest of the region, the city has witnessed an increasing number of sea arrivals and this has produced a demand for reception, support and service provision in the involved provinces of Palermo, Agrigento and Trapani. Between 2017 and 2018, the renewed agreement with the Libyan government have caused a drop in arrivals, and the Law 113/2018, known as Salvini Security Law, produced a steep increase in the number of irregular statuses and the end of many reception and integration projects. Social workers describe these changes as very tangible: the presence of newcomers was reduced and became much less visible. However, while other Sicilian cities, as Catania, are no longer major crossroads, Palermo remains a 'base point'; indeed many interviewees report that nowadays few people arrive directly from the sea, but many keep being transferred from other regional cities, some stay, some come back after having left.

3.2.1 Lights and shadows of an open political discourse

Immigration has become, since the late 1990s, a core and identity theme for Palermo. The Mayor Leoluca Orlando, first elected in 1987 and in charge until 2022, promoted a pro-immigration political narrative, at a local, national and international level. The promotion of a multicultural discourse can be read in relation to Palermo's urban and regional history; it has represented indeed a way to introduce a new and different narrative, also shifting from the long Mafia/anti-Mafia period that had fostered a violent and autarkic image of the city (Bully, 2022). At the same time, this discourse has allowed Palermo to dialogue with international and large cities network working in the same directions and claiming the relevance of the local dimension when dealing with migration. This became evident at the turn of the 2010s through a series of formal recognitions and acts; among others, the institution of the Council of Cultures (Ita. *Consulta delle Culture*) and the Palermo's Chart, respectively in 2013 and 2015.[19] The first was conceived as an elective body, aiming at representing the different ethnic groups and cultures in the city, a tool of democratic participation for immigrant residents. The Chart of Palermo, starting from an international meeting held in Palermo, promoted the principle of human mobility as an inalienable human right. On the same line, in most recent years, local action has been somehow reshaped around the 'welcoming city' project (Bully, 2022): while concerns on migration processes were growing internationally, Palermo has become a reference in the national and international debate for the declared openness toward migration. Internationally, it dialogued and entered large metropoles networks of welcoming cities, promoting the rights of people on the move. Nationally, the Mayor Orlando made a strong opposition to the securitarian policy of the Minister of Interior Salvini in 2018 and often publicly contrasted his discourses. In the occasion of a visit of Matteo Salvini, the former Minister of Interior, to Palermo, the Mayor declared "here there are no migrants, we are all Palermitan (people from Palermo)."

Such a discourse[20] toward migration has certainly opened and secured a space for the growth of initiatives of various kind, however also produced certain contradictions, at least on two levels. As Annalisa Giampino[21] argued, Palermo is really a city full of contradictions; it can be everything and the opposite of everything at the same time. To understand this city, it is necessary to read in the gray spaces, beyond clear-cutting definitions. A first contradictory aspect regards the relation of this policy field to other critical policy fields, such as that of housing. The openness toward migration went hand in hand with the construction of sound relationships with those actors able to realize reception, especially some major third-sector actors that would manage reception facilities or dorms. This collaboration often facilitated and was the base for the construction of public policies – and the distribution of resources often allocated in larger amount to reception project rather than to other fields. This externalization regards, for instance, the public dorms system, which was recently implemented with PON Metro (National Operative Program) 'Città Metropolitane' 2014–2020 funds, a Euro-national investment fund for sustainable urban development,[22] and through a close collaboration between the Welfare Department and the Istituto Don Calabria. In this sense, scholars from the University of Palermo (Giampino, Lo Piccolo and Todaro, 2018) warn about the risk of losing some clarity and transparency in the way policies are built. The well-structured system of actors, which for 30 years has been developing and collaborating with the administration, allows for a high degree of collaboration but also risks preventing a true interpretation and answer of changing needs, especially those that are not only related to immigration. A second contradictory aspect involves the actual impact that the pro-immigration political discourse has had on integration and arrival. Operators and activists point out the gap existing between the political discourse of openness and how services are designed and organized. A very debated example is that of the mentioned Council of Cultures, founded in 2012 as an elective body, aiming at giving representation to immigrant communities in Palermo. Despite this body still exists today and its aim touched the central issue of representation of migrant people, its actual role has been described by many as emptied of a true meaning. By interviewed members of immigrant groups and some Council members, this body is referred to as unable to truly represent ethnic groups; it mainly carries out cultural initiatives, with a symbolic rather than advocacy role. A different case is that of the Registry Office (Ita. *anagrafe*), which has been at the center of a heated debate on the procedure of registration (Ita. *iscrizione anagrafica*) release to newly arrived migrants. In 2018 the Salvini Decree prevented asylum seekers to get this registration, instead Orlando issued an order in the opposite direction, according to the guidelines of the Chart of Palermo. However, the executive directives in the Registry Office did not follow this order and the actual procedures turned out to be very complex.[23] And here lays the contradiction of a city that is willing to be 'welcoming' but lacks the resources to do so.

3.2.2 A composite public action around reception and landing

The development of public policies around migration issues took shape at the intersection of the mentioned political discourse and in relation to existing actors and initiatives. This way of dealing with arrivals can be inscribed within an 'Italian way' to address issues related to immigration more in general, which has been defined as 'local and adaptive' by Tosi (Briata, 2014). Against the lack of a coherent policy framework on a national level, there is a general devolution of functions to local administrations; the latter often delegate themselves, more or less explicitly, functions to third-sector associations to deal less visibly with a problematic issue to the eye of the public opinion. It results a very 'local' way of dealing with immigration, which the delegation to third-sector actors renders also quite 'adaptive'; in Palermo, scholars argue that "the policies for migrants are those self-produced by the associative networks" (Leone, 2013, p. 95). Immigration in Palermo is addressed by a network of actors and power relations that have started developing since the late 1980s and keeps being relevant until today. The diverse actors at stake build a composite public action, where the notion of public must be kept quite broad. When interviewed,[24] Francesco Lo Piccolo warned "be ready for a very broad definition of what is 'public,' here." Around social issues, and particularly immigration and arrival, different dimensions are at play: a public institutional dimension, the active network of third-sector associations and an 'informal' dimension. The civil society, long-term immigrants and their communities, and more recently arrived migrants, play a role and act in this framework.

Large third-sector associations have flourished in Palermo and always had a central role in immigration management. Since the first arrivals in the 1980s indeed Catholic associations have been concerned with newcomers and have often anticipated and solicited the public administration on these themes. Today, in Palermo there is a sound network of third-sectors actors: many are large national institutions – mainly Catholic as Caritas, Centro Astalli, Istituto Don Calabria – some others are smaller and local associations well rooted in the territory. Throughout the years, the relation of these associations with the territory and their reciprocal collaborations has strengthened,[25] as well as their relation with the local administration; many have had and continue having contracts and partnership agreements for the provision of public services. The third sector also includes a range of local and smaller associations, little or not relying on public funds, well rooted in the territory and particularly in the city center. They have often emerged around unanswered social needs, quickly adapting to them, and in many cases end up filling the gap left by the local administration – as it became clear with the increasing arrivals starting from 2014 and with the recent social and sanitarian crisis. In this regard, it is worth mentioning the religious institution *Missione Speranza e Carità* founded by Biagio Conte in 1991 to host homeless people around the central station. Today it includes nine structures in the province of Palermo, hosting up to 1,000 homeless – among whom also migrants: five times the number of hosts of public dorms. The role of this institution is very debated: whereas the living conditions of its hosts are in most cases very poor, these structures have been a crucial buffer and containment of a huge social demand that the public administration has not been able to address. Next to older associations have recently emerged smaller groups explicitly addressing migration issues and human rights; they mainly promote advocacy activities and support initiatives for migrants and often work within sound networks. During the pandemic, the role of these actors has come dramatically clear, a volunteer of the Centro Astalli argued that "without local associations, in the city center a war would have broken out" (Cecilia M., Italian operator at Centro Astalli).[26] On the one hand, their action proved necessary, and, on the other hand, there has been a high risk of substitution of the public actor. Interestingly, in recent years there is an increasing number of formal and informal groups composed by recently arrived migrants who come together to support and advocate for their own rights – Stravox and Jekafò are two of them. Unlike older immigrant associations, they do not group according to their nationality, but rather around common aims and claims. They are still very young experiences; however, they are also expressing the need for self-representation, which is often harder to find in the above-mentioned third-sector actors.

Finally, immigration and landing intertwine with a broad and plural realm of non-institutionalized actors, ranging from co-national subletting rooms and providing job opportunities to the mentioned illegal trafficking networks. The role of these actors varies according to different factors; the bond with the local co-national community is often strong in the case of people coming from Bangladesh, in many cases newcomers can find a temporary accommodation at co-national places and share some job opportunities until they reach autonomy. For other newcomers, as Africans, the bond with older immigrants might not be as strong. As mentioned, informal – although very well-organized – actors include trafficking networks, as in the case of prostitution where are often involved young Nigerian women who move within well-established international networks raging from central Africa to Palermo and up north.

3.2.3 Old and new spatial patterns

Already in the first decade of the 2000s, Lo Piccolo and Leone (2008) underlined the importance of the spatiality of immigration in Palermo. Particularly in the city center – between the inner areas of Ballarò, Capo, Zisa, the Station and the Cala, on the seaside – since the 1970s, immigrant groups have distributed themselves with further distinction.[27] Although in Palermo we cannot talk about closed 'ghettos,' national communities settled in distinct urban areas. Starting from 2015, landings have outlined new spatial pattern (Bovo, *forthcoming*). A first one, strongly linked to recent landings is that of reception facilities; in line with the national framework, larger reception centers – often CARA or CAS – have been located in the outskirt of the city or in bordering municipalities of the metropolitan area. The work of Bully (2022) addresses their distribution and organization, highlighting a 'two-fold spatialization of reception spaces' in Palermo: the city core with practices of reception developed by third-sector actors and the Municipality, and reception facilities in peripheral areas. A second pattern includes all those places out of the reception system, which however work as infrastructures for landing. Interestingly, despite some institutional spaces, such as the police immigration office, public clinics and helpdesks, or the already mentioned private dorms, many realities managed by smaller third-sector associations concentrate in the core of the historic center , i.e. the Ballarò area. The historic center was already a popular neighborhood before World War II, laying south the richer area of Libertà. Strongly damaged by bombings during the war, the historic center was definitively left aside also by the after-war urban developments, which involved new peripheral areas (Bully, 2022). Since then, the historic center has represented one of the poorest areas of the city and still does today; here Italian families coexist with long-term immigrants, and all often live in very degraded housing conditions and work in a secondary market, as the pandemic outbreak has clearly showed.[28] Since few years now, this area has been more and more dwelled by young activists, originally coming from more bourgeois areas, and slowly starts being object of touristic activity. The area is defined as the heart of Palermo, with a strategic position. The resulting concentration of immigrant population, newcomers, new services and activism initiatives renders the historic center and, particularly Ballarò, a very peculiar context. However, some are critical about such a concentration, admitting that the problem is now how to get out of the center, that is described as a black hole. The operator of a local helpdesk for migrants describes it as

> a ghetto, where communities have a role in structuring the paths of those who arrive; the Nigerian community for example engulfs you, there are people who have been here for 20 years and do not know a word of Italian, because Ballarò allows you to do that.
>
> (Sara A., volunteer of the association Ikenga)

Interestingly, there are realities that explicitly attempt to move from there, even only by moving few streets away, as the Ikenga Association, or the public office of the Casa dei Diritti, whose location however sometimes is perceived as far, as that of the schools CPIA (Provincial Center for Adult Instruction; Ita. *Centri Provinciali per l'Istruzione degli Adulti*).

In this sense, the area of Ballarò has some of the features of arrival neighborhoods, whose resourcefulness grounds on the offer of – mostly informal – job and housing opportunities (Lo Piccolo and Leone, 2008) and the concentration of support services and activities. Interestingly, unlike other Italian cases (Bovo, *forthcoming*) in this neighborhood, immigrant residents not necessarily play a role of 'brokers' (Hanhörster and Wessendorf, 2020) for newcomers who rather find infra-national support networks among each others and local activists or service providers. In conclusion, we may argue that the issue of immigration fits within the complex context of Palermo, intertwines with the history of the city and shapes its current identity. For various reasons – also spatial ones – immigration has never caused huge social tensions; however, it has expressed the contradictions of a city officially open to foreigners but constrained by structural obstacles. In this sense, the image of a porous and sponge city seems to fit well: a city with a general low social control that absorbs the new, for better or worse.

Notes

1 This two-fold principle was established by the Schengen Agreement, signed in 1985 and progressively implemented in the following years – see the Maastricht Agreement, signed in 1992 by Belgium, Denmark, France, Germany, Greece, Ireland, Italy, Luxemburg, the Netherlands, Portugal, Spain and the United Kingdom.
2 Despite smuggling and trafficking are often overlapping, the two terms underline a difference. The first refers to the situation when individuals pay someone to facilitate their travel across countries; here, there is a consent of migrants in the migration process. Trafficking instead implies no consent or that consent is obtained through coercion, deception, threat or use of force; trafficking includes prostitution, forced labor, slavery and similar practices (Monzini, Nourhan and Pastore, 2015, p. 13).
3 Renown emblematic examples were the Albanian arrivals in southern Italian coasts and migrants crossing the Strait of Gibraltar toward Spain.
4 With the term 'mixed migration flows' we may intend

> a movement in which a number of persons are travelling together, generally in an irregular manner, using the same routes and means of transport, but for different reasons. Persons travelling as part of mixed movements have varying needs and profiles and may include asylum-seekers, refugees, trafficked persons, unaccompanied/separated children, and migrants in an irregular situation.
>
> (Monzini, Nourhan and Pastore, 2015, p. 13)

5 This term is used in Algeria and Tunisia to define young citizens who are leaving the country through the Mediterranean; the term literally means 'burned/burning' and refers to the route that is burned by these young nationals, or to the burning of their documents before the travel.
6 Activist of Alarmphone Watch the Med.
7 When referring to the migration processes, asylum policies – more than generic immigration policies – assume relevance and will be particularly addressed.

8 The Bossi-Fini Law (L. 189/2002) established the largest regularization in the Italian history – with 701,906 requests and 90.5 percent of approvals. The last one occurred during the pandemic, in 2020.
9 As it shows the Law Minniti-Orlando (L. 46/2017) and the following Security Decree, by the Ministry of Interior Matteo Salvini, in 2018 (D.L. 113/2018), changed by the next Ministry Lamorgese, in 2020 (D.L. 130/2020) – where asylum is a central topic.
10 The data in this subsection are mainly referring to research and elaboration of the Fundation Openpolis and the Italian Institute for Studies of International Politics (ISPI) – among other references their last report (ISPI, 2021).
11 The program, introduced with the 2020 reform, replaces the System of Protection for Holders of International Protection and Unaccompanied Foreign Minors (Ita. *Sistema di Protezione per titolari di protezione Internazionale e per Minori stranieri non accompagnati*) (SIPROIMI), established by the Security Decree in 2018, which replaced the System of Protection for Asylum Seekers and Refugees (Ita. *Sistema di Protezione per Richiedenti Asilo e Rifugiati*) (SPRAR), in force from 2002 to 2018.
12 On January 2021, the total number of migrants hosted in reception facilities of all kinds was 80,097 (Openpolis, 2021).
13 In the same year, Italy registered a little less than 120,000 disembarkations and a little more than 130,000 asylum requests (Frontiere, 2018).
14 On this point, it is worth recalling the work of Fontanari (2019) and its protagonists' life experiences.
15 In their 2016 Report, the Naga association in Milan (2016) – historically working with migrants – describes the reception system as the Goose Game, where one can be lucky and go through the whole system, or suddenly be pushed back to the beginning. Additionally, the work of Elena Fontanari (2019) and the experiences of her research protagonists are examples of this 'limbo.'
16 An example is the issue of access to housing, which represents in Europe a key difficulty for migrants exiting reception projects.
17 In 2011, Palermo had 29 percent of unemployed over its population, in line with those of other southern Italian cities – Naples had 26 percent – and much higher than northern Italian contexts, as Milan that in 2011 had 6 percent.
18 Interviewed in Palermo by the author on September 29, 2020.
19 Lo Piccolo (2013) also mentions the URBAN program, through which the Municipality attempted a dialogue with immigrant communities. Later the Strategic Plan of 2010 included among its guidelines and keywords the 'city of integration', although this risked not to be coherent with the executive actions, but rather a rhetorical record.

20 In 1984, Secchi (1984) discusses the role of discourses and practices in housing policies.
21 Professor at the Architecture Department at the University of Palermo interviewed by the author on October 20, 2020.
22 The city of Palermo has benefited from this program since 2014 and which has financed, among other things, mobility projects or major urban requalification, but also hospitality initiatives (Bully, 2022).
23 The complains of activists and migrants led Orlando to declare he would sign himself the registrations to the Public Registry of the city if the Office wouldn't have done so.
24 Interviewed by the author in Palermo on July 23, 2020.
25 In Palermo, the collaboration between different associations began to be established already in the 1990s, through shared experiences on the theme of childhood and experimental regulations promoted in those years (Law 285/1997). In an interview, Claudio Arestivo, co-founder of MoltiVolti, states that many people within the Ballarò network have been working together since then and keep doing so until today (Bovo and Galimberti, *forthcoming*). More recently, the so-called refugee crisis has also been a further reason of collaboration and so has the pandemic.
26 All names of interviewees had been changed to preserve anonymity.
27 Official data do not reach such a small scale, however these geographical patterns are well documented by qualitative research as the one presented by OMA in the Manifesta Biennale, 2018, and were confirmed in the interviews conducted in this work.
28 The pandemic outbreak has showed how many Italians in this area do not have residency documents and thus had major issues in accessing municipal aids, for the same reasons of many immigrant newcomers.

References

Baroni, C. (2019) *La ḥarga: migrazione clandestina tunisina in Italia, cause e caratteristiche*. Sapienza Università di Roma, Rome.

Borderline Sicilia (2019) *Tunisia porto sicuro? Storie di violenze e deportazioni dalla frontiera tunisino-libica*. www.borderlinesicilia.org/tunisia-porto-sicuro-storie-di-violenze-e-deportazioni-dalla-frontiera-tunisino-libica/

Bovo, M. (forthcoming) "Changing geographies of landing in Italy. Migration movements and spaces in contemporary Milan and Palermo," in Templin, D. (ed.) *Arrival neighborhoods: Migrations, urban spaces and infrastructures in European Cities since the late 19th century.* New York: Routledge.

Bovo, M. and Galimberti, B. (forthcoming) "Preparedness: spunti di riflessione dalla teoria e dal campo," in Giampino, A. and Todaro, V. (eds.)

Transizioni post-pandemiche Crisi ed evoluzione della urbanistica nell'era post-Covid. Milan: FrancoAngeli.

Briata, P. (2014) *Spazio urbano e immigrazione in Italia. Esperienze di pianificazione in una prospettiva Europea*. Milan: FrancoAngeli.

Bully, É. (2022) *Palerme, «Ville Accueillante»? Instrumentalisation politique de l'accoglienza, formes d'hospitalité locale et effets sur les trajectoires des exilés*. Université Paris-Est, Paris.

Cellamare, C. (2011) *Progettualità dell'agire urbano: processi e pratiche urbane*. Rome: Carocci.

Ciabarri, L. (2015) "Dynamics and representations of migration corridors: The rise and fall of the Libya Lampedusa route and forms of mobility from the Horn of Africa (2000–2009)", *ACME*, 13(2), pp. 246–262. Available at: https://acme-journal.org/index.php/acme/article/view/1006 (last accessed on December 26, 2023).

Colucci, M. (2018) *Storia dell'immigrazione straniera in Italia: dal 1945 ai nostri giorni*. Rome: Carocci.

Corrado, A. and Colloca, C. (2013) *La globalizzazione delle campagne, Migranti e società rurali nel sud Italia*. Edited by A. Corrado and C. Colloca. Milan: FrancoAngeli.

Cremaschi, M. and Lieto, L. (2020) "Writing Southern theory from the global North. Notes on informality and regulation," *Equilibri*, 24, pp. 261–280. doi: 10.1406/98117

del Grande, G. (2023) *Il secolo mobile. Storia dell'immigrazione illegale in Europa*. Milan: Mondadori.

Ferrario, P. (2014) *Politiche sociali e servizi: metodi di analisi e regole istituzionali*. Rome: Carocci.

Fontanari, E. (2019) *Lives in transit: An ethnographic study of refugees' subjectivity across European borders*. London: Routledge.

Giampino, A., Lo Piccolo, F. and Todaro, V. (2019) "Questione abitativa e diritto alla città a Palermo," in *Transizioni post metropolitane. Declinazioni locali delle dinamiche posturbane in Sicilia*. Milan: FrancoAngeli, pp. 185–214.

Greco, S. and Tumminelli, G. (2020) *Migrazioni in Sicilia 2020*. Milan: Mimesis.

Grillo, V. (2016) *Border perspectives on migration policies: Refugees in Tunisia*. University of Vienna.

Hanhörster, H. and Wessendorf, S. (2020) "The role of arrival areas for migrant integration and resource access," *Urban Planning*, 5(3), pp. 1–10. doi: 10.17645/up.v5i3.2891

Hess, S. and Kasparek, B. (2017) "De- and restabilising Schengen. The European border regime after the summer of migration," *Cuadernos Europeos de Deusto*, 56, pp. 47–77. doi: 10.18543/ced-56-2017pp47-77

ISPI (2021) *Le migrazioni nel 2021*. Milan.

Leone, D. (2013) "Palermo: la multietnia chiave di lettura della città postmoderna," in Lo Piccolo, F. (ed.) *Nuovi abitanti e diritto alla città. Un viaggio in Italia.* Florence: Altralinea Edizioni.
Lo Piccolo, F. (2013) *Nuovi abitanti e diritto alla città: un viaggio in Italia.* Florence: Altralinea Edizioni.
Lo Piccolo, F. and Leone, D. (2008) "New arrivals, old places: Demographic changes and new planning challenges in Palermo and Naples," *International Planning Studies*, 13(4), pp. 361–389. doi: 10.1080/13563470802519030
Lo Piccolo, F., Giampino, A., and Todaro, V. (2018) "Non profit per chi? Riflessioni sul ruolo del Terzo Settore nella costruzione di una nuova politica per la casa a Palermo," *Urbanistica Informazioni*, 278 s.i., pp. 76–80.
Medici Senza Frontiere (2018) *Fuori Campo*. Rome-Milan.
Mezzadra, S. (2004) *I confini della libertà. Per un'analisi politica delle migrazioni contemporanee.* Rome: DeriveApprodi.
Migreurop and FTDES (2020) *Politiques du non-accueil en Tunisie. Des acteurs humanitaires au service des politiques sécuritaires européennes.* Paris and Tunis.
Monzini, P., Nourhan, A. A. and Pastore, F. (2015) *The changing dynamics of cross-border human smuggling and trafficking in the Mediterranean.* Rome: Istituto Affari Internazionali.
Naga (2016) *(Ben)venuti! Indagine sul sistema di accoglienza dei richiedenti asilo a Milano e provincia.* Milan.
Natter, K. (2019) *Political regimes and immigration policymaking: The contrasting cases of Morocco and Tunisia.* Amsterdam Institute for Social Science Research (AISSR).
Openpolis (2021) *Centri d'Italia, una mappa dell'accoglienza.* Rome.
Paluzzi, P. (2017) "'Sbarchi fantasma' dalla Tunisia, la nuova rotta dei migranti," *ANSA*, 6 October. Available at: www.ansa.it/sito/notizie/mondo/2017/10/05/ansa-reportage-sbarchi-fantasma-da-tunisia-la-nuova-rotta_4 5153206-ff17-49fa-9d1b-9b67f391c014.html (last accessed on December 26, 2023).
Picone, M. and Schilleci, F. (2019) "Una postmetropoli incompleta: il contesto socio-spaziale di Palermo," in Lo Piccolo, F., Picone, M., and Todaro, V. (eds.) *Transizioni post metropolitane. Declinazioni locali delle dinamiche posturbane in Sicilia.* Milan: FrancoAngeli, pp. 163–184.
REACH and Mercy Corps (2018) *Tunisia, country of emigration and return: Migration dynamics since 2011.* Geneva.
Secchi, B. (1984) *Il racconto urbanistico: la politica della casa territorio in Italia.* Torino: Einaudi.

4 Urban spaces as landing infrastructures

After outlining the main traits of the context of Palermo, we will assume a closer gaze on the city, unpacking how ordinary urban spaces work as landing infrastructures. At a local level, the city can be seen as offering a set of grips and resistances that channel the everyday lives of landing migrants. These can be read through the concept of 'infrastructures' as those places newcomers get entangled upon landing: dorms, helpdesks, health clinics, public offices and public spaces. The notion of 'infrastructure,' as used in interdisciplinary literature (Klinenberg, 2018; Meeus, Arnaut and van Heur, 2019), underlines the channeling function of these places as platforms of arrival and take-off, keeping their materiality and relational nature together. Drawing on the recent debate, we will assume an elastic notion of landing infrastructures, remaining open to investigating where and how landing occurs. To do so, we will primarily focus on spaces, starting from the spatial dimension of landing infrastructures and assuming the city of Palermo as a field of observation, through a progressively zoomed-in look. What are the trajectories of who lands in the city? What geographies do emerge? What are the features of these spaces?

4.1 Plural uses, plural spaces

To answer these questions, a premise is necessary: people finding themselves in the condition of landing in Palermo, even in the same years, experience very different situations, have profiles that change and keep changing within short time periods and can be described as different populations. The net of political discourses, policy measures and local initiatives we described are some of the external factors influencing these experiences, for which also individual choices have an impact. In this sense, we should be aware that the populations who land are different and so are their competencies of use of the city and the trajectories and spaces they get entangled with. Let's consider some examples. Some migrants, after arrival, spend in Palermo only a few hours or days and after disembarkation reach the station to leave the city. Maghrebi, and all those whose country of origin is considered 'safe,' usually get a rejection note (Ita. *foglio di via*) and are "left to their own destiny," as Rahim K. (Moroccan mediator at the helpdesk Arci Porco Rosso) states.[1] These people often aim at reaching France or other European countries and, thus, directly head to the train station. For some, transit might last a couple of days; in this case, they look for a safe place where to leave their stuff and sleep, a place where to have breakfast or take a shower the day after, sometimes they also look for money transfer services.

Together with 'transiting' migrants, there are people who, with or without a rejection note, leave Palermo to reach rural areas to enter the agricultural labor market. Often, they join acquaintances in the peripheries of rural towns like Borgo Mezzanone, Campo Bello di Mazara or further. During winter, when seasonal work stops, they might return to Palermo, use temporary accommodations, shower and breakfast services, sleep in dorms and wait for the next agricultural season. In the latter case, people on the move experience circular mobility and a fragmented temporality.

Among landing migrants there are also those who are entitled to ask for asylum and enter the institutional reception system. Their landing continues into reception facilities, mainly CAS (Extraordinary Reception Centers; Ita. *Centri di Accoglienza Straordinaria*), often located out of the city (Bully, 2022). In these structures, people happen to spend months or even years, often isolated from the city life; operators take care of administrative, sanitary and legal procedures. Buses and trains connecting these places to the city become major resources. Some structures are so far that it takes hours for people to walk to Palermo, and making the round-trip often takes more than the available free hours allowed by centers, as explains Andrea A. from a Borderline Sicilia Onlus. Other reception facilities, more often SAI (System of Reception and Integration; Ita. *Sistema Accoglienza Integrazione*), are located in the urban area; in these cases, people still spend a lot of time in the structures and operators 'mediate' their contact with the city, by taking care of sanitary, administrative and legal procedures for them. However, in these urban facilities, migrants more easily get in touch with volunteers and external associations, and they can leave the center during the day.

As we have seen, reception facilities host only a part of newcomers arriving in Italy; those who find themselves out of institutional reception take different paths: some leave the city, and others choose to try and stay in Palermo, with or without a valid residence permit (Ita. *permesso di soggiorno*) – because "at the end of the day, here, you manage to survive" (Laura A., Italian volunteer at Centro Astalli). Landing trajectories, in these cases, intersect and get entangled with a range of different places: people start looking for housing solutions, as Taijib M. (operator for the helpdesk InGioco) explains, many share flats, "you may find an apartment for 200€ and share the coasts." Or, as it more often happens in the Bangladeshi community, "you live by an acquaint, or family member, and find a small job – as roses seller or street vendor – to share the expenses, before trying to move by your own" (Syed G., Bangladeshi mediator). This is also what people arriving in Palermo from other cities may choose to do; indeed, "sooner or later, everybody lands in Palermo" (Rahim K.) also because there are services and support networks. People who remain in Palermo after arrival use sanitary services, bureaucratic help desks and public services where to follow legal and administrative procedures, public spaces where to simply spend free time and Italian classes. At this point, people see what happens, how things evolve; some manage to find a job, get their documents and find support in local associations, and landing may eventually give the way to the intention to permanently settle. This is the case of Rahim K., who arrived in 2005 in Palermo, from Morocco, and finally chose to stay, or of Bayo B., who arrived from Gambia in 2015 and, despite he initially meant to reach an English-speaking country, today is a cultural mediator and works at Arci Porco Rosso; he has a partner in Palermo and has chosen to stay – at least for a while. Others, instead, may not find a job or may have been waiting too long for documents or have friends elsewhere and choose to leave. This is the case of Ibrahim L., a Ghanaian mediator I met in Palermo in July 2020, who soon after left for Germany. This is also the case of many Bangladeshis who more and more often move to Portugal, as Syed G. told me while sitting in front of Teatro Massimo, in the city core. Finally, many, after having left, return and land once more in Palermo. Each of these populations use the city in a different way and outline geographies that sometimes are unique – like those of reception facilities – and sometimes overlap between each other and with those of local and more permanent residents (*see* Figure 4.1).

4.2 Geographies beyond planning logics

To further understand how landing spatializes, we will have a walk through the landing spaces that are more recurrent in the words of the interviewees encountered in the field. We will be able to outline a geography of landing and discuss how this often does not match the logic of the arrival neighborhood or urban and social planning logics (*see* Figure 4.2).

4.2.1 The trade-off between quality and access: public and private dorms

Among all landing spaces, the first and more recurrent one in the words of migrants, mediators, operators and policy makers is definitively *Biagio Conte*, i.e., the name of the lay missioner who founded in 1991, the *Missione Speranza e Carità*. The Missione, as mentioned, is a religious community that manages a series of structures for homeless people in Palermo. The Missione has three main structures in the city, one for women and two for men; the largest is in the southern area of Palermo, few kilometers south the train station. After a slight turn from the main street, it seems to enter a small village with very precarious low houses, where people sit on chairs and check the street, as in rural towns not used to visitors. At the end of the road, a brick wall opens in a gate; some bikes are locked on nearby light posts, and people sit behind the gate and chat. This dorm was a former National Air Force warehouse. Today, it includes a vast unpaved outdoor courtyard with two big trees; the dorms are in two long buildings facing the courtyards. Next to them, other buildings host the canteens, kitchens, toilets and laboratories where missioners make bread and artisanal objects and a huge church. Furthermore, empty buildings and outdoor spaces are still under renovation; next to this area under construction, the border wall lowers, showing traces of jumps: mattresses on the two sides work as steps to help the climb and descent.

I eventually managed to visit the Missione on a hot Tuesday in July; Alberto R., whom I contacted, invited me to the morning mass in the central headquarters of the Missione; there, I would have met Biagio Conte and then walked with Alberto R. to the nearby dorms in via Decollati. If I had to describe that day, I would say that

88 *Urban spaces as landing infrastructures*

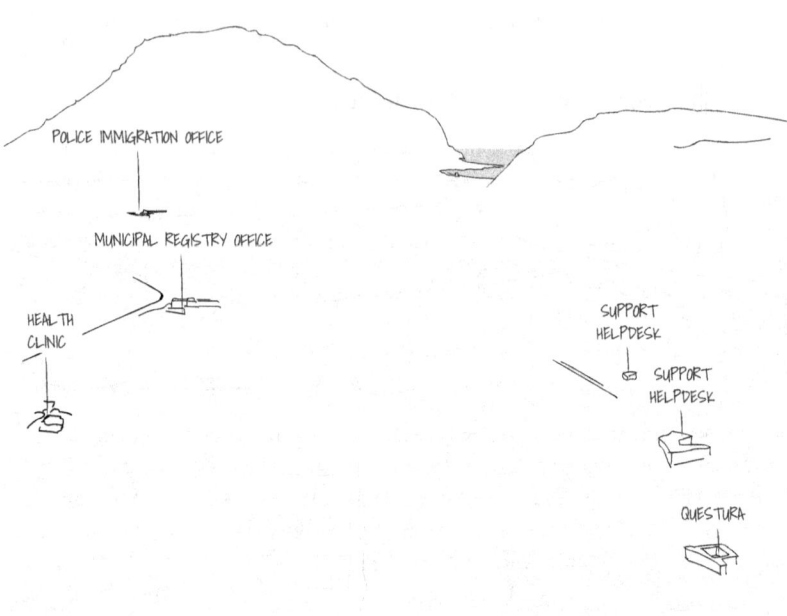

Figure 4.1 Spaces of landing for 'those who stay': a look from above. Drawing by the author, 2021.

Urban spaces as landing infrastructures 89

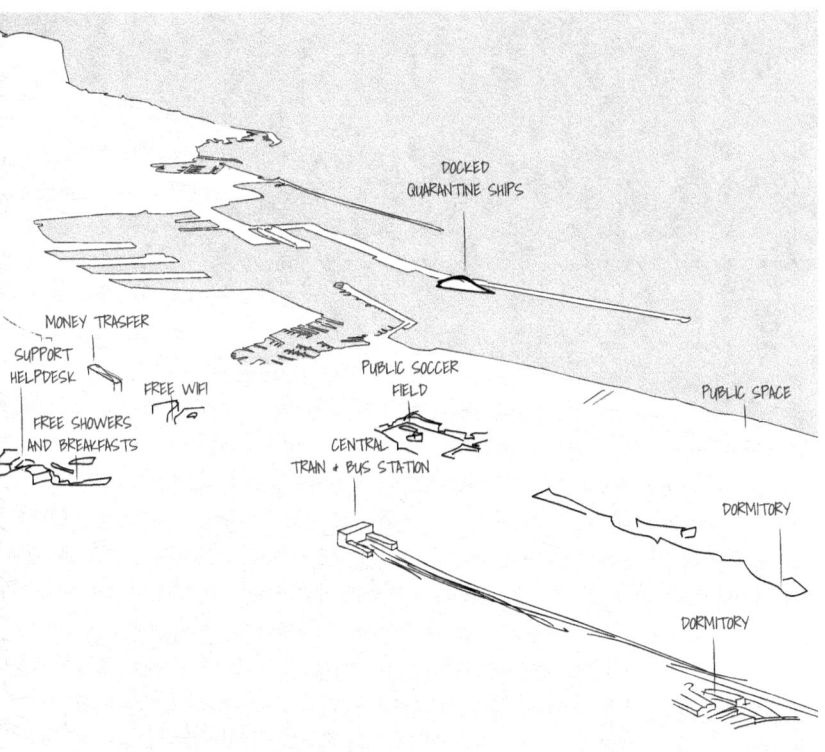

90 Urban spaces as landing infrastructures

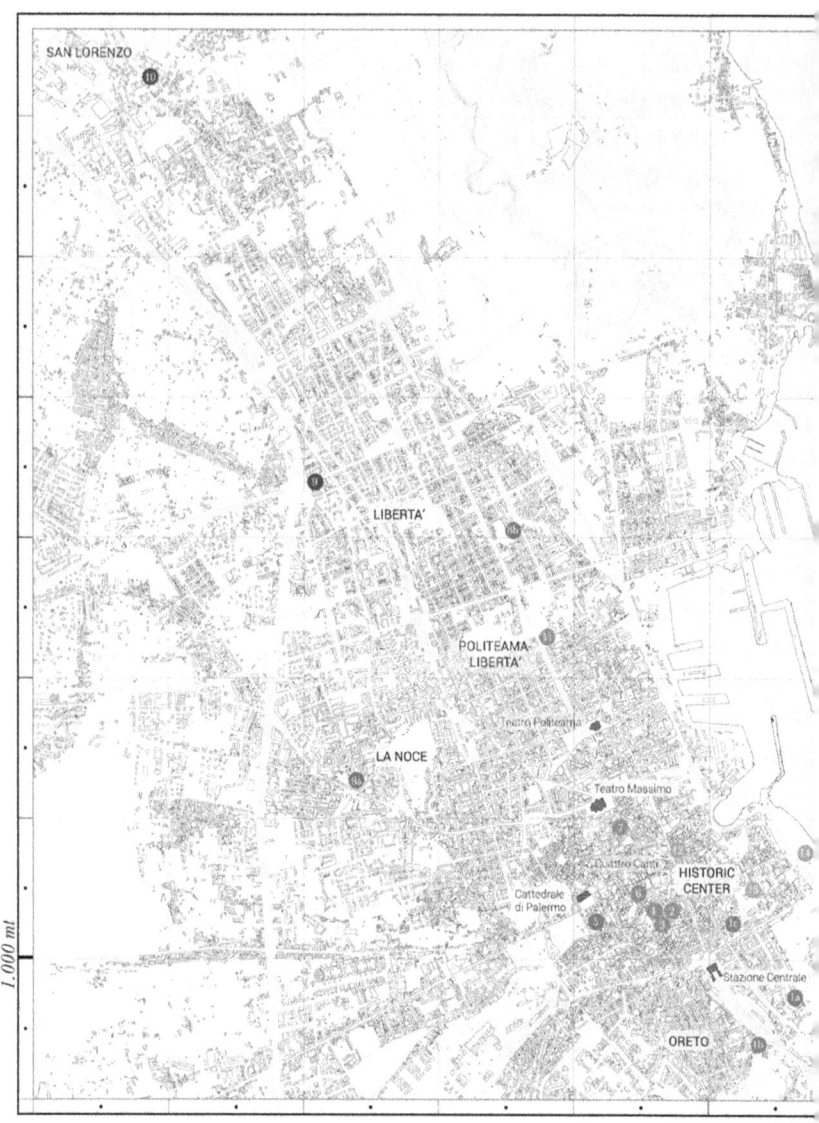

Figure 4.2 The geography of landing spaces: a walk through. Drawing by the author, 2021.

Urban spaces as landing infrastructures 91

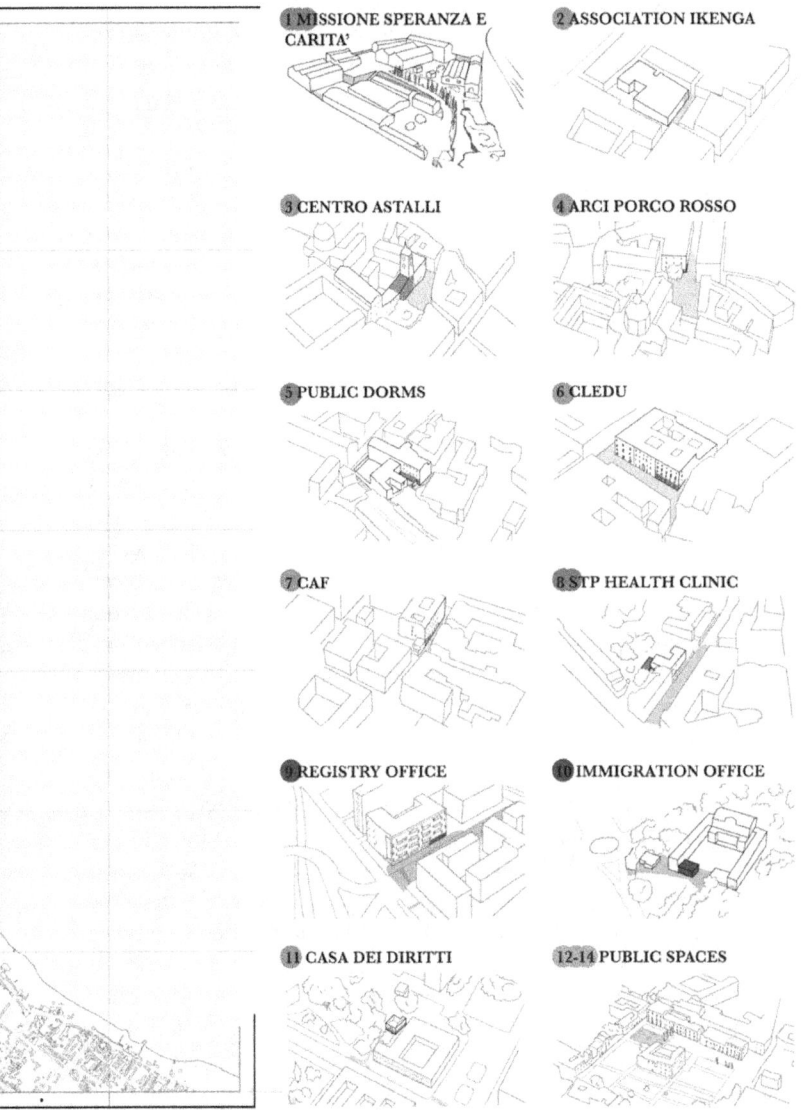

starting from 7:30 am when the mass started, I entered a 'narrative bubble' and felt all the contradictory nature of that place. The visit was filled with generous descriptions of details and information about the church's history, the authors of paintings and sculptures, and the laboratories where missioners would print small images of saints – however, not a word of dorms and the hundreds of people living there. While listening, I saw a man sitting near a fountain, talking to himself, picking up stones. While leaving, I sincerely thanked Alberto R. for his availability; he indeed was kind to walk me for a whole morning through the Missione and show me what he could, but for some reason, I was left with a feeling of discomfort, how was possible to describe that space without saying a word about its hosts?

(Fieldnotes, July 2020)

In Palermo, everybody mentions the Missione but always with mixed feeling, many with a resigned tone – as if they 'had to.' These dorms indeed host more than 1,000 people in the face of the 200 total beds of public dorms: what they contain is in the first place the housing emergency of the city. Public actors acknowledge this role, "they manage to do things that the Municipality does not [..], without these structures, people would simply live in the street" (Roberta L., Italian social worker at a public helpdesk); and Biagio Conte has a strong role in the Municipality: "he is everywhere, if he fasts[2] everything keeps still, you can't move a step" (Roberta L.). Additionally, the main dorms are the most accessible facilities in the city, as they allow for an easy access and exit. People go there and are let in, with no access procedures, nor waiting list, nor limitations in the staying; Rahim K. told me "You know how it works there? The border wall is low, and people simply jump in and out of the dormitories." This is the big difference with public dorms that instead require a longer entrance procedure and set maximum staying periods.[3]

However, the resigned tone is also there: the dorms are described as mere 'containers – in the sense that contain' (Amal Y., volunteer at MoltiVolti), 'no more than parking lots' (Roberta L.), where homeless people stay. The living conditions in these dorms are often problematic to the point that some would compare them to spaces with a very negative reputation: "is a very bad place, as the Libyan detention centers; a guy who has been sleeping there for two months, while waiting to enter a reception facility, could not believe that that was in Europe" (Taijib M.). Here is the mixed feeling and resignation: a trade-off between access and quality. On the one hand, a broader access and ways of access that better suit populations with a circular mobility and, on the other hand, a very controversial quality of the same offer.

4.2.2 Along the border and inside the neighborhood of Ballarò

We now move past the train station walking up north, along the large viale Roma. On the right, between other small streets, we find the space of the association Ikenga. One of the many associations is located in the historic core of Palermo; they are however not yet in the inner area of Ballarò, from where they explicitly chose to remain 'out,' or "at least beyond via Maqueda" (Sara A., volunteer of the association Ikenga), out of a 'black hole' mechanism that they argue is more and more common in Ballarò. Ikenga is a cultural association belonging to the national Arci network[4] held by volunteers and providing at times helpdesk services; on their Facebook page, it says, 'always open,' and indeed, at any time of the day the two doors of this 'informal space,' as the founder would define it, are open. On the chairs, randomly positioned on the sidewalk, there is always someone sitting and chatting (*see* Figure 4.3).

Figure 4.3 The Ikenga association. Photo by the author, 2020.

As we walk a hundred meters west, we enter the inner area of the historic center: Ballarò. Here, as Francesco Bellina[5] says, integration takes place at 360 degrees, both in the positive and negative sides. Not far from Ikenga, we encounter the Centro Astalli,[6] recurrent in all answers on relevant landing spaces: mediators from all countries, local migrant associations, social operators, the Welfare Deputy Mayor of Palermo, everyone mentions it. After a narrow street, it opens a small square full of cars. The square is overlooked by a building of the XV century; on the ground floor of this building, a small open door is the entrance of the Centro Astalli that offers free breakfasts and showers every day. Toilets and showers are accessible from a corridor behind the entrance counter; on its right, instead, there is a room that remains open and available for the whole day. Here, there is a couch, available power sockets and a water fountain – as those you often find in Italian public squares. "You know, in dorms or at Biagio Conte you don't get to sleep the whole night through, you need to watch for your stuff; so, people come here during the day, charge their phone and simply rest" (Cecilia M., Italian operator at Centro Astalli). In the other spaces of the building, on the two upper floors, there is a bazar of used clothes, a laundry service, a health ambulatory, classes where they teach Italian, a general support service and a legal helpdesk. Stella A., a doctor volunteering at the center, defines it 'an open door with free access.' Rahim K., while mentioning how a usual day could look like for a person in the process of landing, says people "in the morning [often] go to Centro Astalli, to have breakfast and take a shower." Indeed, every morning at 9 o'clock, doors open, and the center offers an average of 90 breakfasts a day during winter; while in summer "people usually are not in town, they leave for seasonal jobs, and the center provides approximately 40 breakfasts a day" (Cecilia M.). Showers are also available, and every day around 40 people use this service in the morning and other 40 in the afternoon. At lunchtime, the doors close, although a staff member always remains inside and opens them back in the afternoon until 7 pm. The Centro Astalli is the first of the many associations that are located in Ballarò and among whom there is a continuous exchange.

We continue our walk, and past the square, we take a left into a narrow street; here, doors on the ground floors often lead to the so-called *bassi* (Eng. lows), i.e., apartments that lay under the street level. After heavy rains, as the one witnessed in Palermo on July 15, 2020, you would see people emptying their houses with buckets full of water. At the end of this street, another square opens, piazza Casa Professa. Here is where the Arci Porco Rosso association is located, only few steps away from the Centro Astalli, and few steps away from MoltiVolti, the Senegalese association, the Santa Chiara Oratory and the Caritas, all realities that in different ways work with people with a migrant background. This association is often mentioned and attended by African migrants; here, on Wednesday's afternoon, the *Sans Papiers* helpdesk gives support to documented and undocumented migrants and Italians with bureaucratic and legal issues. The Arci Porco Rosso occupies a small ground floor space, on the corner of a residential building: a door facing the square and another door facing the side street (*see* Figure 4.4). People pass by and see what is going on; this visibility is crucial for volunteers: it makes things easier respect to other spaces that are not so visible. As the CLEDU (Legal Clinical for Human Rights, Ita. *Clinica Legale per I Diritti Umani* – a legal helpdesk), that before the pandemic used to take place in a room inside the Department of Law of the University of Palermo, not far from the Arci. Here, differently from the Porco Rosso, people needed to enter the main hall, ask the gatekeeper where the CLEDU

Figure 4.4 The Arci Porco Rosso helpdesk. Photo by the author, 2020.

was and then follow indications and signs until they would reach the right room. Although this association is mentioned by many migrants and local operators as a reference, not everyone uses it extensively; for instance, while African people, through word-by-mouth, often come here, Bangladeshi rather use other kinds of services, as Syed G. would tell me. Interestingly, before the pandemic outbreak, many Asian migrants found the CLEDU more welcoming. "There, you had a more precise place, lawyers, the access was more direct" (Seyed G.). In Ballarò, we would also find some of the city public dorms, and they are hardly noticeable from the outside; only a careful eye would recognize the tags on the wall mentioning the Italian funding program PON Metro and the European Union symbol.

We start leaving Ballarò, and, via Maqueda, we pass through street vendors, some fancy shops, people chatting and walking, tourists eating. Here, if we pay attention to the shop's signs, we detect money transfer and 'Asian services.' These are the CAF Patronati (Centers of Fiscal Assistance; Ita. *Centri di Assistenza Fiscale*) run by people with Asian origin and mostly – but not only – attended by Asian migrants, mainly Bangladeshi. Almost at the end of via Maqueda, we take a left and find another Asian Service. Here, as Kazi A., the owner and member of the Intercultural Council of Palermo, explains, they provide support with bureaucratic procedures, job contracts and legal documents, many of these services are charged. A small ground floor space, with a big window on the street, these spaces look like ordinary offices: two chairs in front of a desk, a computer and some papers on it and a person sitting on the other side. In this CAF, approximately 70 percent of the clients are Bangladeshi, others are Africans or Chinese. Here, as Seyed G., argues "the approach is different," people are 'clients,' unlike the Arci associations for instance, and this sometimes meets better the people's needs. During the day, Asian services working as CAFs are always busy. Kazi A.'s CAF opens at 9 am; however, already from 8:30 people arrive and sign in the waiting list. This happens in an interestingly and hardly detectable way; to an uninterested eye, indeed, there is no visible line nor waiting list. People approach the closed shutters of the CAF and take a small piece of paper hanged and hidden on a corner, they write their names on a list, fold and put the paper back and wait until the owner arrives and open the shutters and the office.

Walking back to via Maqueda, up north, we end up in piazza Teatro Massimo, where the main theater – the *Massimo* – of Palermo overlooks a large square. Along the sidewalks facing the main facade of the theater, street vendors give way to elegant touristic cafes and fancier shops. Palm trees decorate and make some shadows on the large open space facing the beautiful stairs that lead up to the main entrance, the perfect background for wedding pictures and Saturday afternoon. Piazza Teatro Massimo is mentioned by many as 'a fixed meeting place' (Seyed G.).

The recurrence of this space in the words of newcomers reminded me of a work I did in Milan, with migrants hosted in first reception facilities. During interviews they would repeatedly mention going in their free time to piazza del Duomo, the central square hosting Milan's cathedral; this somehow surprised me, I probably thought that piazza del Duomo was a place only for tourists. Instead, I later realized that when I happened to live in foreign cities, I also found myself spending time in such places, simply because they are easy to discover, open to all, and beautiful.

(Fieldnotes, July 2020)

In piazza Teatro Massimo, people cross the street from all sides, some simply wait, some others sit at cafes and chat, some wait at the postal office on the southern corner of the square. This is also a crossroads, where the core part of the historic center ends and a more bourgeoisie area of Palermo starts.

4.2.3 Temporality and healthcare: clinics as places where to feel 'safe'

At this point, we head to a very relevant landing space, one that is mentioned by many, especially by mediators and migrants, namely the clinic *Aiuto Materno*.[7] Walked past Teatro Massimo, we come across the area of the Capo Market, where migrants with Asian origins have settled, we pass by Palermo's Court, keep walking aside the area of Zisa toward the more peripheral neighborhood of La Noce. The district is characterized by a large building discontinuity, limited on the one hand by the ring road and closed south by the Zisa area; originally a rural area, it is today one of the most densely populated districts. Here, after a 30-minute walk from piazza Teatro Massimo, we encounter the clinic Aiuto Materno (Eng. Maternal Aid) (*see* Figure 4.5). It is a generic and public ambulatory, which, besides carrying out general medicine functions open to all residents, is also specialized in

Figure 4.5 The public health clinic Aiuto Materno. Photo by the author, 2020.

dealing with foreign patients. This specialization is developed in two different ways: on the one hand, this clinic as only other few in Palermo issues the code for Temporarily Present Foreigners (Ita. *Stranieri Temporaneamente Presenti*) (STP); on the other, it offers cultural mediation, social and medical support. The STP code gives access to essential and urgent care to people without a valid residence permit, who cannot sign in the national health system, nor be assigned to a general practitioner. Ibrahim L. explains that "for a person who newly arrived is crucial, because it makes you feel safe." Not by chance, when I interviewed him, this was the first space he mentioned and where he insisted to walk me. Also Bayo B. and Seyed G., the founders of an Islamic Women associations, the volunteers of the Arci and the lawyers of CLEDU, refer to the sanitary field as a field that works well for landing. There are other first access and urgent care services, as the *Guardia Medica* and the First Aid (Ita. *pronto soccorso*); however, often communication represents a problem and affects the actual accessibility to cares.

In the same area there is the office of a general practitioner who works with newly arrived migrants. Newcomers with a valid residence permit have access to the national health system and therefore to an individual general practitioner (Ita. *medico di base*). Ibrahim L., while walking toward the health clinic Aiuto Materno, told me the name of a few doctors he would generally suggest migrants to contact. One of them is Mauro S., who works in a clinic in the area of La Noce. His ambulatory is in a residential building; as for many Italian general practitioners I have happened to see, the ambulatory is an apartment: the living-waiting room, a couple of bathrooms and other rooms where doctors have their offices. Doctor Mauro S. explains that in Palermo, general practitioners who take charge of newcomers are few, and some have a lot of patients that often reach them for their location or through word-of-mouth. This is not a work for all:

> once, a young man, rang the bell asking for 'Mario', that after a while we understood meant 'Mauro' – myself. Then, he entered my office and directly crashed on the bed in front of my desk, took off his shoes and complained about being tired.
>
> (Mauro S.)

He underlines that there are cultural barriers that need to be overcome to understand and deal with such behaviors, and not all are ready to do that. When I was in his ambulatory, properly sitting on the chair in front of his desk, he showed me the file of a young migrant, born in 1997, who was assigned to him but had a valid permit of only one month, so he would have had him in charge only for 30 days. This gives an insight into the openness of the landing process – I thought – and the difficulties to deal with it. This is why STP clinics are so relevant: the STP code and cares are delivered right away to people that often have more certainties about the present and fewer about their future.

4.2.4 Exclusion and inclusion in public offices

We eventually leave the neighborhood of La Noce, and head north toward viale Lazio, where the Municipal Registry Office (Ita. *anagrafe*) is. Here, we are in a different area of the city, larger roads and higher buildings. The Registry Office is located at the northern border of the area of Libertà, an area of residential expansion developed between the end of the XIX and the beginning of the XX century, that is until today one of the richest of the city. The Registry Office is another of those landing spaces that people mention because they 'have to'; here indeed, after having received a permit by the Immigration Office, migrants ask for the municipal registration (Ita. *iscrizione anagrafica*). This allows to sign a job contract, a rent contract, to open a bank account – a possibility that may sound banal but is not at all.

> *Every morning the office opens at 8:30 and closes at lunch time. Due to COVID19 restrictions, the waiting space was moved on the sidewalks facing the office's entrance, red textile bands dividing the space into two corridors, one for foreign requests and another for nationals. Here, two men in uniform answer people's questions, showing them where to queue and call the names of those allowed to enter. On the whole sidewalk, there is almost no shadow and no proper place to sit; the lucky ones end up sitting on empty flower pots on the street. Those with an online appointment waited for their name to be called, while others had to wait in line. Initially, services for migrants couldn't be booked online, and foreign people were forced to queue outside the office; "people would arrive at the office at 5 am, to start queuing. Once, I arrived at 7:45 am and was already the 54th in line, at 1 pm only nine people had been let in," once told me two lawyers of the CLEDU. Inside, around an empty central space with some chairs, deploy a U-line of counters, with glass windows dividing operators from users; only two of them are used for foreign requests, the number 3 and 5. Here, a very kind operator, Andrea, tries to answer and deal with all kinds of requests.*
>
> (Fieldnotes, September 2020)

Despite the relevance of the services issued by this office, confusion and inefficiency characterize it and often result in exclusionary practices. A social worker, asked about these offices, argues

> the point is that some rights, such as registry rights, are fundamental. However, beyond a political narrative of the Municipality, the offices in charge of ensuring these rights have highly discriminatory modes of access. Request for residence that lasts up to eight months does not mirror human lifetimes of people. In this sense there is a real difficulty in guaranteeing fundamental rights.
>
> (Roberta L.)

Urban spaces as landing infrastructures 101

Figure 4.6 The Police Immigration Office. Photo by the author, 2020.

Out of the Municipal Registry Office, we head further north, to the Police Immigration Office. To reach it, we must take a bus. The Office is in the neighborhood of San Lorenzo, around four kilometers from the Registry Office and seven kilometers from the city center. This area, originally known as '*Piana dei colli,*' (Eng. plain of hills), hosted several villas, that however with the great urban expansion after the World War II, got mostly occupied by apartment buildings and lower warehouses structures. As we ride, the landscape out of the bus window changes, residential buildings get less and less dense; the Monte Pellegrino, the hill overlooking Palermo, seems closer and closer. After approximately 15 stops and 20 minutes, we get off in via San Lorenzo Colli, near the Immigration Office (*see* Figure 4.6). Here, people take appointments and withdraw their residency permit; thus, in front of the gate, where they are asked to wait, we would find migrants who have been living in Palermo since decades, as Robert, V. who I met waiting to withdraw his renovated five-year residence permit and those who are fixing the very first appointment of the long asylum request procedure. Despite the disorganization, this Office has a central role for people in the process of landing, because "the first problem, in any case, are documents" (Bayo B.). Also in this case, the way the service is organized and space regulated is often producing and reproducing exclusion and temporariness of landing migrants. Here people come several days a week, sometimes receiving documents only after the expiration date. This episode, drawn from my fieldnotes, gives an insight into such situation:

> *Abbas S. arrives from the office and takes his bike, they ask him if he had solved anything, his answer is negative. He will have to come back tomorrow with the appointment. The answer triggers some irony among others. Robert V. comes back from his appointment, and with his big surprise, tells us that everything went well and shows us the residence permit. "It will last until 2025!" He is really surprised that it took only three months to have it renovated, last time he had waited a year. He says that often, upon withdrawal, the permit has already expired, but you have to pick it up anyway to renew it. John sees Robert V. with its permit on hand and asks "Did you pass the exam? Did you get merit (Ita.* lode*)?" "I'll pass it but without merit, mine will only last one year."*
> (Fieldnotes, October 2020)

It is time to go back to the city center; on the way back, at the end of a small and green street, we gaze a two-floor liberty building; here is where the *Casa dei Diritti* (Eng. House of Rights) is. It is a municipal office started in 2018 and located in this space in 2020, short before the pandemic outbreak, when all the projects stopped and "everything went up in smoke" (Ita. *"tutto s'affumò"*), as argues the social worker in charge of the office. The Casa dei Diritti aims at coordinating diverse services addressing the foreign population in Palermo, mediating among municipal services and third-sector actors. The space, open to users, was meant to host diverse realities working with foreign inhabitants, not only to promote networking among these realities and a public coordination but also to offer everyday different helpdesk activities – such as job orientation by SEND, the helpdesk of Refugees Welcome. In other words, this office is where the Municipality does all those the things that other offices do not, or cannot do. The social workers of Casa dei Diritti were repeatedly mentioned by operators and volunteers of the Arci, of the Centro Astalli, of the STP clinic Aiuto Materno. This service work as a sort of background infrastructure, not only offering direct support to users but also supporting operators of other services. Interestingly, it provides an alternative example of what a public office could look like, how it can make a different sense of a service and a space (Weick, 1995).

4.2.5 Public spaces as infrastructures

We leave the nice liberty building and take the bus again, heading south for a couple of stops. In the historic center, there are some public spaces that many mentioned, in such a way to underline that in Palermo there are also beautiful places, where one can simply walk, talk, play soccer, make calls with the free Wi-Fi or wait for the day to be over. Getting off the bus next to the Quattro Canti, we walk down via Maqueda, on our left piazza Bellini that, thanks to the free Wi-Fi, fills up with people in the late afternoon. In piazza Magione, that opens into a wide-open space, on a corner there is a soccer field, free and public, where I have always seen people playing and others watching and waiting to play. I have been told, indeed, that here also migrant newcomers go very often. Leaving piazza Magione, as we walk toward the sea, out of La Kalsa, we cross a large, trafficked road we eventually reach that public space facing the sea, the Foro Italico (*see* Figure 4.7). This is a space mentioned by many and it is

Figure 4.7 The Foro Italico. Photo by the author, 2020.

a particular one. It consists in a large open space, partially covered with grass and partially paved, unfolding along the sea, near the touristic harbor of Palermo. All kinds of people walk, some run or ride a bike, some play soccer and other kinds of sports, some sit and teenagers walk. Here is also where the final day of the Ramadan is celebrated, and where parts of the Cavadee rituals of Mauritian and Tamil populations took place (Viani, 2019). The Foro Italico appears to be, not only a landing infrastructures but a social infrastructures (Klinenberg, 2018), a place that affords for social interactions; a place where written and unwritten social and spatial rules are loose enough to render the coexistence among strangers possible (Anderson, 2011).

4.3 The space as physical setting and object of regulation

The encountered infrastructures broadly differ in nature. However, they all offer affordances for landing and shape the everyday lives of newcomers and their access to urban resources. The reasons why they are, in most cases, supporting landing lie in some features they share: their continuous presence and openness, their accessibility and flexibility in use. To better understand these features, we will now zoom in on three different infrastructures and reflect on how their spatial settings and regulations are organized. Drawing from Bifulco's (2003) work, we will discuss the space's role in shaping interactions, activating contexts for action and owning a generative potential. They present some spatial variables that often mirror how associations and institutions work: among others, visibility, thresholds and borders, functional specialization or looseness and aesthetic quality.

4.3.1 The Immigration Office

The first infrastructure we will observe is the Police Immigration Office. In Italy, under the Ministry of Interior and in each province, the Questura represents a local body of the National Police with a technical and operative role. The Questura deals with issues of public order and security, coordinating local police forces. The Police Immigration Office belongs to this large institution and to its Immigration Department that deals with immigration under a security perspective; namely, the Departments' Chief of the Police

Immigration Office and its operators deal with arrival and disembarkation operations, photo-signaling, interviews and issue of residence permits and ID documents. Newcomers disembarked in Palermo and willing to ask for asylum, to declare their willingness to stay, need to go to the Police Immigration Office and ask for an appointment. It follows a complex procedure, where several appointments must be fixed over time, to officialize and receive a temporary permit of six months – while waiting for the Territorial Commission decision upon the asylum request. To this complex mechanism, we should add the already mentioned unclearness and disorganization that characterizes these procedures in practice.

> The problem is the 'arbitrariness' with which these things are done, everything depends on the person on duty, on how he feels that day [..] Depending on the operators inside, *anything can happen to you*, there are no established rules or practices, there is no stable procedure.
>
> (Eleonora G.)

Waiting times are also a major issue, sometimes for a temporary residence permit of six months validity, people wait three months for the withdrawal; an appointment asked in October might be fixed for the following January. Newcomers are required to make use of this infrastructure, which however seems to mirror and amplify securitarian and exclusionary approaches of national and international migration policies.

As we have seen, the Office is located quite far from the city center; passed a large entrance for cars and the staff, the entrance for users of the Police Immigration Office becomes visible in front of a roundabout (*see* Figure 4.6). Nothing tells that this is an entrance to the Immigration Office. On the right a high concrete wall covered with metal spikes prevents any crossing, only few fallow plants fill the voids among the spikes. In front of the widest part of the sidewalk, it opens a six-meter-long metal-bar gate with a narrow door; on the left, the wall covered with spikes continues and the sidewalk gets narrower again (*see* Figure 4.8). In front of the gate, an unpaved area of less than 50 square meters interrupts the sidewalk and faces the roundabout. Behind the gate, two gazebos, and at around 50 meters distance, the main yellowish building of the Police Immigration Office.

106 *Urban spaces as landing infrastructures*

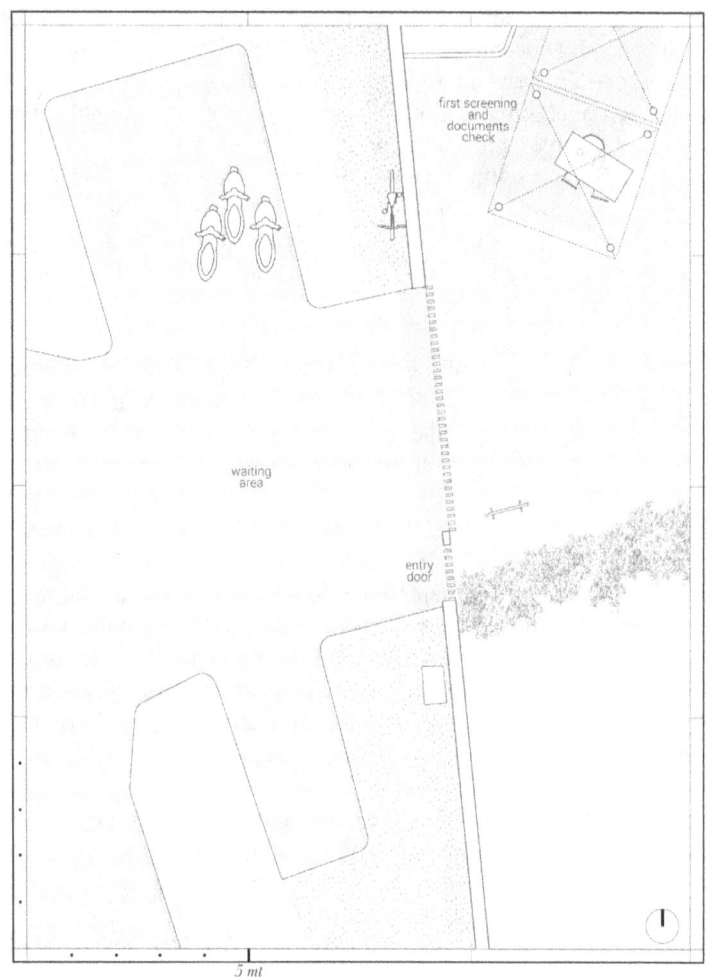

Figure 4.8 Plan of the Immigration Office's waiting area. Drawing by the author, 2021.

From Mondays to Fridays, from 8 am, people start gathering in front of the gate (*see* Figure 4.9). It is not a real line, but rather a random group of people standing on a broken sidewalk in front of the roundabout. Many line along the concrete wall, not because there is a seat but simply because a small stripe of shadow still covers that part of the sidewalk.

There are people of all kinds, southern Asian young girls with colorful dresses chatting, as if they were spending their free time in a public square, but with a bitter expression on their eyes; mums that play with their children, old people on wheelchairs, young black men standing and greeting each other, Chinese people, nuns, families. Almost everybody holds papers, documents in their hands, carefully gathered in plastic or paper covers. Closer to 8:30, people keep walking from the station and the bus stop, some arrive on motorbikes that can be heard approaching – even before you see them – and park in front of the gate. Some get dropped off by cars.

(Fieldnotes, July 2020)

Little after 8:30, the guards appear next to the door, together with few cultural mediators. At their appearance, people get closer to the gate, some hand in something. There is a mess, and it is not easy to understand how things work. As a girl explained to me, first you must hand in your paper to the mediators, then you simply wait until they call your name; you enter, pass through the door, get through the 'check in' procedures under the gazebos behind the gate and then walk to a courtyard of the main building. There you wait again until it is your turn in the offices; eventually, you leave from the main entrance, the one with the palm trees. In the meantime, an increasing number of people start approaching the gate; those who are 'new' to the place tend to gather in front of the gate. Time passes by and the sun gets warmer, almost everyone moves along the wall, under what remains of the shadow – the only one except from that under the gazebos on the other side of the gate. Some people look for a seat: there is no bench, nor chair, nor flowerbed: the most comfortable seats are the step of 20 centimeter between the sidewalk and the street level, or two broken pieces of stone laying under the wall, on the right of the gate. Eleonora G., volunteer at the Arci Porco Rosso helpdesk, when talking about this experience of waiting, describes it as a matter, or a test, of 'physical endurance.' A general sense of powerlessness prevails.

The tension gets higher, once I heard a woman in perfect Italian complaining, "I've been here under the sun since 8 o'clock, they told me to come on the first useful Wednesday, if there is no office

Figure 4.9 A morning at the Immigration Office. Drawing by the author, 2021.

Urban spaces as landing infrastructures 109

> number, how am I supposed to know what to do?", and the mediator behind the metal bars of the gate answering "I'm a mediator, I just take the paperwork, here the office opens at 8:30, it's useless for you to come at 8 o'clock"; still on a perfect Italian and with a Palermitan accent, a man on the phone "he [the mediator] took the list, obviously there is the usual chaos." Instead, 'regular users' wait a bit further, as if they knew how things work: there is no need to stand close to the gate, until they start calling names.
>
> (Fieldnotes, July 2020)

Eventually, mediators start calling people's names; they get repeated, in search for the right person, until one starts running to the gate. It is hardly believable how within that mess, people manage to hear and distinguish their own name and surname, that is probably wrongly pronounced. Each time the mediator approaches the gate, all – also the most frequent users – get closer, to hear what he says or to hear what other people repeat after him; moving too far or sitting along the wall under the shadow is impossible now: you must see the mediator approaching the gate, step closer and hear the name he pronounces. People enter through the doors one by one, pass by the guards, along a crash barrier (Ita. *transenna*) and then turn toward the gazebos, wait in line and in line leave toward the second courtyard. As Robert explained, in 2019, after a dispute between a mediator accompanying a person and the staff, no external people have been allowed, only those with an appointment can enter, one by one. In the meantime, waiting continues, people chat, exchange information and news; irony, mutual help and listening appear to be the main defense mechanisms to face this confusion. Finally, around lunchtime people start leaving, the place gets emptier and emptier until the next morning.

In the attempt to understand how this infrastructure channels landings – even if not supporting them, – it clearly appears the role of space, both as a physical setting and an object of regulation. Drawing from Bifulco's (2003) contribution, we can underline some aspects of it. First, the space of the Immigration Office is clearly functionally specialized, and

> the specialization of the spaces of the organization releases its generative force first of all on the structuring of the relations that take place there, on the subjects that these relations deal with, on the place that different figures are required to occupy. And it is

precisely the observation of this physical specialization that helps to understand how a service can produce its own object.
(translation by the author; *ibidem*, p. 33)

In the Immigration Office, the space is organized and ruled so to create a clear distinction between who is allowed to be inside and who is required to wait outside. On the one hand, those entitled to give the access to regularization procedures in its different steps: the guards opening the doors, the mediators calling their names or the officers processing their documents, and above all Territorial Commissions choosing on their asylum requests in the framework of national and international directives. On the other hand, undocumented people who, though their presence there, confirm their condition and need to behave accordingly. Power relations are very visible, the need to stay close to the gate to hear names that are called, the absence of clear timetables, waiting times are all means of affirming such power relations. On a micro-scale, this is what Fontanari (2019) describes as the production of fragmented temporalities, in her *Lives in Transit*: procedures that prevent to have full control on personal lifetime but constrain people's everyday life to the timing set by blurred and often intentionally unclear bureaucratic procedures. Such an organization is strengthened through further artifacts: the gate marking a close border, the absence of aesthetic quality – or even comfort. Bifulco (2003) underlines the role of borders and the extent to which thresholds can be crossed and lie in continuity with the surroundings. Here the threshold is very sound: the wall is high and covered with spikes, the gate is always closed and the door opens only to let people in, one by one. The access is physically organized and regulated so to prevent free entrances and exits, instead to control and select. Finally, the lines: once crossed the gate, people line up, following the bureaucratic chain of paperwork and steps to reach the internal offices – as de Leonardis (2001) writes about lines, "the impression is that the figure of the line constitutes a basic metaphor for the institutional world" (translation by the author; *ibidem*, p. 102).

4.3.2 A public health clinic

The second infrastructure is the clinic Aiuto Materno; within the local Provincial Health Agency (Ita. *Azienda Sanitaria Provinciale* – ASP) of Palermo, there is an Operative Unit (Ita. *Unità Operativa* – *UO*) for the Promotion of Immigrant Health[8]: this Unit offers health and social assistance to foreigners temporarily or permanently present on the territory. It addresses all immigrants, documented and undocumented, EU and non-EU and their families. The Unit gathers various competences, namely two doctors, a pediatrician, a nurse and a social worker, with the collaboration of a gynecologist, psychologists, social workers trainees and cultural mediators, and consists of two outpatient clinics: the *Centro Salute Nomadi e Immigrati* (Eng. Immigrant and Nomad Health Center) and the clinic Aiuto Materno. The Provincial Health Agency, the Operative Unit and the two clinics are public structures, where the regular doctors and the social assistant are employed as public workers. The access is direct and open to everybody, no reservation or booking is needed. Among the two clinics, the clinic Aiuto Materno was the most mentioned among interviewees and represents the main reference in terms of healthcare for migrants, thanks to the mixed offer of medical and social assistance, that others do not provide, but also to the provision of the STP code (*see* Section 4.2.3). Despite the generalist nature of this service, its specialization on a newcomers and immigrants is evident:

> We are open every day, sometimes even until six in the afternoon. Many people don't go to their general practitioner, even when they have one, because they work and would have to ask for a leave to their employers to go during opening hours. There is a need for flexibility in this sense.
> (Marta E., social worker at the clinic)

To give an idea of the number of users, at the time of my visit, the clinic had 2,549 open files, i.e., patients, only for the social service, and 4,362 social and medical files.

As we have seen, reaching the clinic from the central square of Teatro Massimo takes around 40 minutes. Along the small residential street, the clinic Aiuto Materno can be recognized from the sign hanged on the wall, at the street number 10b (*see* Figure 4.5). On the sign, under the logo of the Public Health Agency of Palermo, ASP 6, we read the name of the Operative Unit for the Promotion of Immigrant Health, and that of the clinic, written in six different languages. On the right are all opening hours and a phone number. A step after, a blue decorated gate is low enough to gaze what it encloses, on its right a ring bell. At opening hours, the blue gate and a glass door to access the clinic remain always open. Out of opening hours, people can ring the bell and ask to access. After the blue gate, a small courtyard leads to the entrance glass door. Plants of various kinds defy the concrete pavement and struggle to grow, nicely framed with stones; others bloom on carefully watered flowerbeds. Before the door, on the left a very tiny light-blue bench offers some seats. On the glass door hanged papers give all kinds of information, about how to respect distancing measures and about changed opening hours or events and language classes.

Outside some people waiting and taking a few steps in and out of the courtyard, the bench rarely is empty, two people often sit very close by. Leaned on the wall a few others, between flowerbeds. Some talk to each other, some look at their phone. I have never seen more than five, six people at a time. People come and go quite quickly; no-one stays more than half an hour. Occasionally, one of the people sits on the tiny bench, stands up, stretches and then sit back, not to lose the precious place. Doctors, mediators, and other operators pass in the inner corridor, sometimes they quickly stop to say hi to who is waiting, the threshold between inside and outside is continuously crossed by people's word, greetings, steps of those entering and then leaving. When nobody is there, the glass door gets closed, while as soon as someone appears in the courtyard, it gets open again, and a person from the inside welcomes in the newcomer. Around six, the courtyard gets eventually empty, from the clinic a person comes and closes the blue gate from the inside.

(Fieldnotes, October 2020; *see* Figure 4.11)

After the glass door, the clinic deploys in a ground floor space, of approximately 150 square meters, divided into several rooms (see Figure 4.10). After the door, a corridor, whose walls are painted in washable dull colors – as those of any social and sanitary public space in Italy – hosts some chairs and leads to three rooms. On the left, a room with two desks is where cultural mediators usually work and on certain days also the psychologist. Before the COVID-19 pandemic, this was also the waiting room. The following door leads to a second room, with a desk and a meeting table, all kinds of chairs

114　*Urban spaces as landing infrastructures*

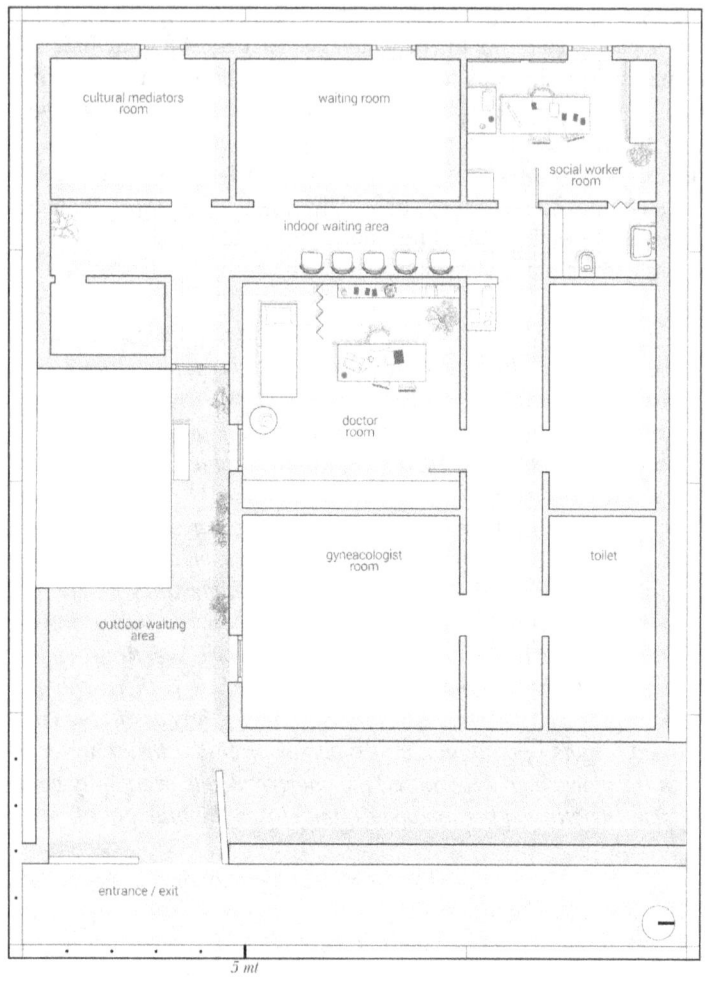

Figure 4.10 Plan of the Aiuto Materno health clinic. Drawing by the author, 2021.

gathered around it; here usually the staff holds meetings and check-in procedures. The third room is the office the social worker; it has a small internal toilet next to the entrance door. On the walls, pictures, notes and drawings tell the stories that lay under the numbers and files

Urban spaces as landing infrastructures 115

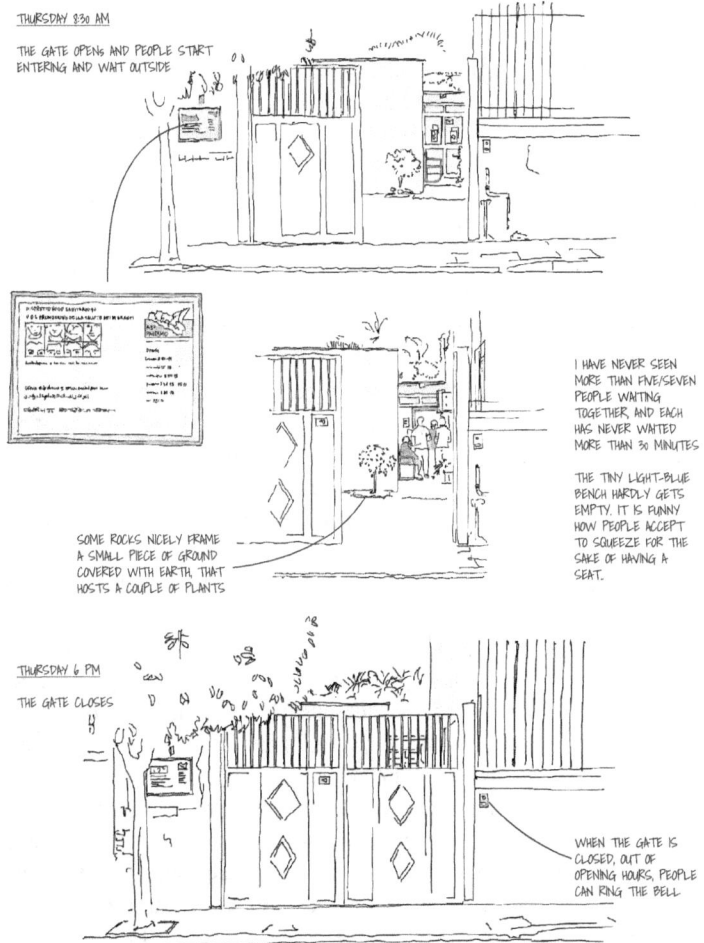

Figure 4.11 Observations out of the health clinic. Drawing by the author, 2021.

she has followed since 1993, when she started working and when – she underlines – was held one of the last public calls for social workers in Palermo. Behind the desk, a window; on the desk, a computer screen, papers and a printer, and in front of it two chairs. Her presence there is fundamental, as it is the bond between the social and medical sphere that reciprocally support each other.

116 *Urban spaces as landing infrastructures*

> *The social worker says that often people go there complaining about a stomachache and then they start finding out all other kinds of social and sanitary issues; this is why having the two competences together makes such a good service: often expressed needs are only parts of the actual ones.*
>
> (Fieldnotes, July 2020)

Out of the room the corridor makes an 'L' and leads to other two rooms and a toilet; the first is that of Doctor Lino, the clinic responsible. It is defined as the 'beating heart of the clinic,' Doctor Lino indeed was there before anybody else and is a reference for colleagues and patients in Palermo. Objects of every kind fill the room: books, posters and paintings on the walls, plants and papers on the desk, traces of use are everywhere. It resembles a private house, if it wasn't for the medical bed, half hidden under a curtain at the end of the room, next to the window. It follows the room of the gynecologist and in front of it a nicely decorated toilet. Back out in the courtyard, behind the bench a small room, they meant to renovate to host Italian classes; however, the project got stopped by the pandemic outbreak and the room remained empty, only stickers on the windows witness a former use.

The organization of this space contributes to the infrastructuring action of the health clinic. Once again, it is interesting to underline how the nature of this service, the clear willingness to adapt to newcomers' needs is enacted through its spaces. As seen, this health clinic is recognized as crucial in the everyday life of newcomers, especially when undocumented, because it meet people's needs – translation, cultural mediations – and because it releases a temporary code that allows for an *immediate* access to healthcare. Despite the space is functionally specialized, it is organized so to leave some space for the unexpected, and it is managed with a certain degree of 'looseness.' The flexibility on opening hours, the offer of diversified kinds of social and medical support are all examples for this. Bifulco (2003) argues that strictly functionally specialized services tend to reproduce spatially their organization, without allowing modifications and addressing subjects as objects of it. Instead, when a certain degree of looseness allows for adaptability of spaces and its evolutions, the spaces themselves become opportunities for actions and reflection of the service, with a generative potential. Despite the health clinic remains limited within an institutional setting, it is recognizable a certain degree of looseness and openness to adaptability of the service. This can be further recognized by the way the threshold is organized and regulated and how objects, as artifacts are used. Borders can be barriers or bridges, and this depends on the physical conditions of openness and rules of access (Bifulco, 2003); in the health clinic, the gate is kept open during opening hours, and its permeability is guaranteed through the bell out of opening hours. Similarly, the way the courtyard and the rooms are furbished shows an effort to give aesthetic quality to the space, to make people feel at ease, even within a public office. The feeling that prevails is that of an effort to make 'other worlds' possible (Meeus et al., 2020).

4.3.3 A third sector helpdesk

Our last observation takes place in the Arci Porco Rosso, in the core of the Ballarò area, in the historic center. The Arci Porco Rosso is a third-sector association, affiliated with the national Arci network; its founders and members are volunteers. Occasionally, drawing from European and national funds, they have managed to hire paid coworkers; additionally, they collaborate with the many local associations, as regards legal, job-search, language assistance, sharing competences and help. The way the Arci Porco Rosso was born is very representative of how new arrivals of migrants triggered young local activists. In 2015, together with the rise of arrivals in Palermo many associations were started in response to this situation, often funded by young Palermitan working in the third sectors[9]; the Arci Porco Rosso is one of them. The association started from four friends, who happened to be back in Palermo – after having had professional experiences in other cities – and to be temporarily unemployed. One day in 2015, one of them, already part of the Arci network and responsible for migration issues, got a call: a group of 10–15 Gambian young men received a rejection order (Ita. *ordine di respingimento differito*) and were in Palermo with no place to go. Grounding on the network of associations and actors in Ballarò, they finally managed to sort out the situation. Starting from this unexpected experience of support, the Arci Porco Rosso was founded at the ground floor of piazza Casa Professa, in Ballarò, as a space of open encounter and support. One of the founders would say, "the nice thing was that the Porco was the only place where you could have a normal conversation, nobody would ask anything, a real open space" (Eleonora S., volunteer at Arci

Porco Rosso helpdesk). The development of the Arci Porco Rosso, and its open character, did not came without difficulties and risks: on a management level, "at one point we had to fix – and hang on the wall – some rules: don't stay behind the counter, don't move the sockets, this is the Wi-Fi password" (Eleonora S.). Volunteers had to find a limit in the relationship with users, to what extent would they have been helpful or not. Today, the Arci Porco Rosso is described as a place of encounter and orientation to services, "a space where to listen, spend time, ask – apparently – useless questions, that may instead reveal to provide very useful answers" (Eleonora S.). It includes the already mentioned helpdesk *Sans Papiers* for undocumented migrants held on Wednesday's afternoon. In the space, they hold events, parties and assemblies besides the general support and encounter activity. Volunteers, that have changed over the years, today include a Municipal Councilor, social workers, interpreters and mediators, in a mix of migrant and local activists. The economic sustainability until today remains an open issue. In these years, in the Arci needs and requests changed a lot and rapidly (Eleonora G.). During the COVID-19 pandemic, the main issue was finding a bed in the public dorms, the access to basic services and showers or canteens – although these are 'new' needs. More in general many support requests regard the legal and bureaucratic procedures linked to residence permit and municipal registration.

The Arci Porco Rosso is one of those infrastructures that concentrate in the area of Ballarò, in a square where next to a baroque church, there is one of the main places of drug dealing of the city center; on the sunlight and at night, young Italians and foreigners take drugs in the small street next to the church, an open and very well-known wound that expresses the dramatic conditions of the district behind the colorful and 'exotic' image offered to tourists. The Arci occupies a 75 square meters space of the ground floor at one of the corners of the square and it has two entrances, on the side street and on the square (*see* Figure 4.12). On the top of the latter, a red sign with the name 'Porco Rosso' renders the small entrance more recognizable, on the right of it, a small wooden bench is fixed on the pavement. Inside, an open space joins three rooms; the first, facing the square, reveals some traces of an 'entrance': a large table on the right of the door, with a chair, a computer screen and a printer resembles a reception desk, that however is too close to the wall to be used for reception. In fact, all members of the Arci, when interviewed, stress that they

Urban spaces as landing infrastructures 119

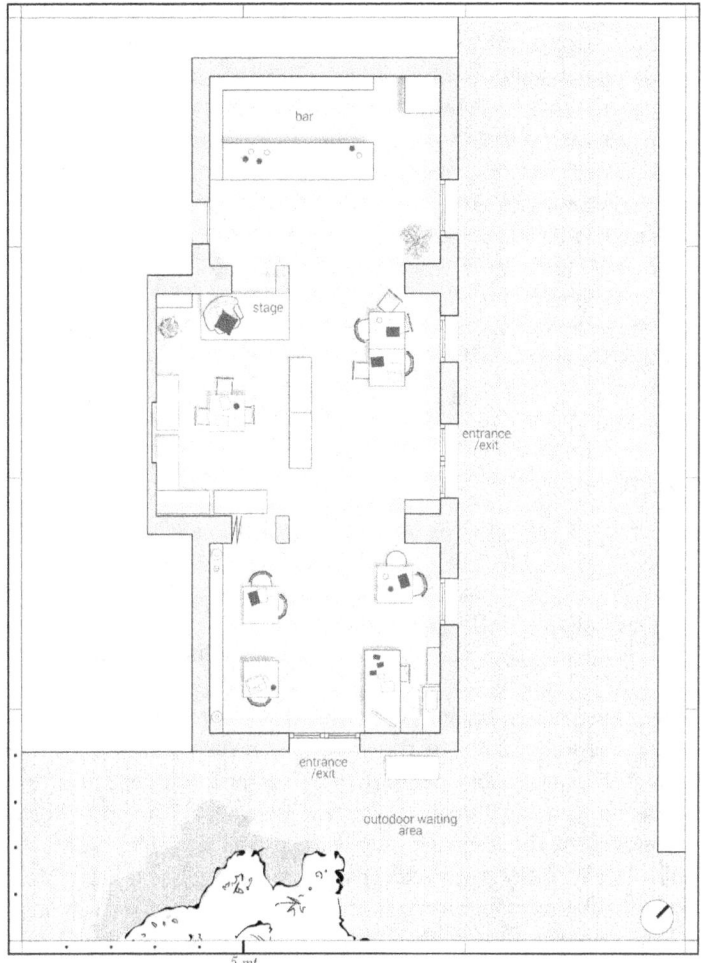

Figure 4.12 Plan of the Arci Porco Rosso helpdesk. Drawing by the author, 2021.

have always refused to have a reception desk or a proper counter – as those in public front-office services: "we never wanted an actual counter, there is just a pen and a desk, so that you can experience it without be subjected to it" (Eleonora G.; Eleonora S.). The second room hosts a small stage, an armchair, chairs and benches. Finally, in the third room, a counter, a fridge and some shelves reveal the diverse uses of this space, which in the evening often hosts public events; on the left a small and hidden door leads to the toilets. The red painting runs up and down on the walls, on the curtains, on the tables' legs and chairs, leaving no doubts on the political orientation of the Arci. Not by chance, the name of the place means 'Red Pork' and is inspired by the homonymous film by Hayao Miyazaki, whose protagonist's motto is *'meglio porco che fascista'* (Eng. better pork than fascist).

Every Wednesday afternoon, the Arci Porco Rosso holds a *Sans Papiers* helpdesk (*see* Figure 4.13). After the staff-meeting, starting from 3 pm, the two doors are left wide open, and people start entering or waiting outside, on the wooden bench and using chairs from the inside. Their presence on Wednesday is a certainty and this represents a key point of this service.

> *Once a south American looking man asked a volunteer how long they would have stayed open and if he could come back at 6 pm, Corrado, the volunteer, smiled and affirmed "you will definitively find us here". And indeed, people keep arriving, entering, and leaving until 7 pm, for the whole afternoon.*
>
> (Fieldnotes, October 2020)

Inside, the space is organized and ruled with great flexibility: 1×1-meter tables joined in the first room for the meeting, start being moved all over the space, and each volunteer sits at a different table with a different person. Some are coupled together so to host broader meetings, instead others are singularly placed here and there, with chairs around them. People enter and progressively sit, members of other associations and public institutions who meet Arci volunteers to talk about forthcoming collaborations, long-term immigrants who have issues with kindergartens for their newborn children or newcomers who did not understand what they have been said at the Immigration Office in the morning. The flow, the movements never stop: people move chairs, tables, their bodies, pens and notebooks, sometimes volunteers reach the printer on the entrance desk and print some papers.

> *While a was there, I found it hard to take notes, I ended up sketching a map of the place and keep drawing small sketches of*

Urban spaces as landing infrastructures 121

Figure 4.13 A Wednesday afternoon at the Arci Porco Rosso. Drawing by the author, 2021.

> what progressively happened at each table, parts of discourses and gestures. On a corner of my notebook, I wrote, "it seems that from each table a room pops up and disappears every time different people sit around it, a room not to be seen but felt."
>
> (Fieldnotes, October 2020)

Such a 'loose' regulation allows for a flexible use of the space: once a young man entered and simply waited on the sofa in the second room for more than an hour. A frequent guest is Peppe, a homeless inhabitant of Ballarò, who occasionally enters from one of the two doors, say 'hi,' and simply sits on an available chair, looking around with a cheerful gaze. However, the little specialization of space requires some 'techniques' to remain sustainable.

On a Wednesday afternoon, between one meeting and the other, Eleonora G. briefly addressed me, she explained that at one point they placed a plastic wall to separate rooms if needed and complains about not having a closed space with more privacy. However, she would choose a corner with benches on the second room, to held more private meeting with vulnerable people, "when women talk about human trafficking, even only having eyes on you is not pleasant," she says. Also, she mentioned that they had to remove alcoholic drinks from the counter because some people freely entering would take them. Indeed, it is hard to recognize who is a staff member and who is not.

(Fieldnotes, October 2020)

People can express very different and often not formalized needs and, out of an institutional setting, the agency of each volunteer is a key point. Sometimes, volunteers ask for reciprocal help, for specific legal or communication and language issues: lawyers from CLEDU pass by, former newcomers now work at Arci as mediators, together with the founders.

Volunteers talk to each other "he does not have a residence permit, but in the meantime we can pre-register him to the CPIA (public schools)". Next to them, an operator says "It depends on where you want to look for work, whether in Palermo or Syracuse. If you live in a place where you can't get mails, you must find one" and then "he has a permit that expires tomorrow for work – When you were in Novara, did you have a contract? Now it's a mess, without a permit you can't find a work contract and without a contract they don't make a permit". Operators move from one table to the other, they listen, try to answer, call for some help and get back to the table, "I summarize the situation: he went to the police station, they told him that two pages for the Commission are not enough, he came back and they asked him to come back with a certificate of hospitality, which they could not ask him – Maybe next Tuesday we can go together to the police station...". While I was there, Corrado decided to personally walk a young man, who had his residency permit expiring the day after, to the nearest trade union to ask for information "I will accompany him now to do the availability for work at the CGL [trade union]" and left.

(Fieldnotes, October 2020)

Everything keeps moving and changing until the late afternoon, until 7 pm; the helpdesk service closes and gives the way to different activities, being them concerts, events or assemblies.

The way the Arci Porco Rosso is organized differs a lot from the previous two places we observed; here, rather than a functional specialization of the space, there is a certain degree of looseness in the way it is designed and ruled. When asked about the reason of the 'success' of the Arci, one of its founder answered "I think because it's an open-access space in a square, it's a little harbor ashore; the level of informality works very much." However, when asked about the difficulties, Eleonora G. adds "informality is beautiful, but you have to do it right." In fact, the lack of a strict regulation and design allows for a great flexibility and adaptability of it and also requires some effort to make it work. On a spatial level, the sense of a harbor, of a controlled looseness, is fostered by details: the 1×1-meter tables make a range of spatial configurations possible, so that they are used for the staff meeting and for individual encounters throughout the afternoon. Seats of different kinds allow for various uses: chairs to sit around the tables, four benches used for assemblies and waiting, a sofa and an armchair. The two doors left open and used on both directions; here, more than elsewhere, the outside comes inside, as if there was no threshold (*see* Figure 4.4). People walk in as if they were walking in the square or on the street and sit on the armchair as if they were on a public bench. About thresholds, Bifulco (2003) writes

> There are services that protect access because they are concerned about the risk of being invaded, first and foremost by improper demands, or because they are oriented to select and discipline users (Centemeri, in this volume). Conversely, there are services that are, so to speak, projected onto their own boundaries, investing

a great deal of activity to make them traversable in both senses: to let people into the physical space of the service and equally to dislocate their services in the surrounding context, say in their own catchment area, for example in the home, or on the street. What happens at the boundaries of the service is an indicator of both the degree of mobility of the service itself and its complementary degree of permeability [...].

(translation by the author; *ibidem*, p. 32)

The Arci Porco Rosso belongs to the second type of services and the permeability of its thresholds allows, in fact, to receive very different kinds of questions – often unexpected. When looking at the space as object of regulation, it becomes clearer how the looseness also requires some control, which is fostered by written and unwritten norms continuously negotiated: on the wall, the written ones forbid to go under the counter, while the unwritten – but well respected – rules prevent the access during the staff meetings. Finally, this also underlines the key role that individuals, especially operators, play when dealing with such a high degree of openness; their discretionary power (Lieto, 2022) matters a lot when navigating such an uncertain environment.

4.4 How does landing spatialize?

We started this chapter mentioning that territories offer grips and resistances to people who are landing. To explore how landing spatializes, setting the spatial dimension of such infrastructures as starting points, we assumed different points of view. A look from above on the overall city, questioning who lands in Palermo and what trajectories they undertake, a walk through the most mentioned infrastructures to understand what kind of geography emerges and, finally, a closer and prolonged look in three of them, to see how they are used and how their infrastructuring work deploys from within. It is worth to draw some considerations on what this adds to the debate on arrival spaces and infrastructures. While sitting for the first time at cafes in the city core and asking the initial questions on *how does landing look like in Palermo* and *what city emerges*, we understood that landings are always plural and so are emerging geographies and cities. Later, when confronted with the representation of the overview, we argued that there is not only one city emerging but many: the Palermo of those who immediately leave, the Palermo of those who take buses toward agricultural areas, that of those who enter reception facilities and that of those who do not. To ground this argument, the work of Crosta (2010, 2018) on the relation between uses and spaces is central; particularly, when he suggests that instead of asking what kind of people use the city, we should question what kind of cities are used by people. This implies that the kind of spaces and infrastructures we identify are not fixed and that should be subjected by a continuous redefinition, always starting from the way people on the move find themselves using the city and on a situated knowledge.

The acknowledgment of the plurality of landings and cities forced us to outline a more precise field of observation, namely urban landing spaces, out of reception facilities, considered relevant for who lands. They are mainly ordinary spaces that for a certain period *also* chanel landing trajectories. . We identified some shared features of those places working as infrastructures, namely those that support the everyday life of migrants without trying to reduce their 'futuring vectors' (Meeus *et al.*, 2020). A continuous presence on the territory, in terms of service provision and in the availability of the space is crucial, especially when dealing with undocumented migrants, who come and go in the city or stay for short periods, and that are usually labeled as temporary. The clear and continuous functioning of these spaces indeed often renders them reference points, known by word-of-mouth and easy to reach especially by those who are not stable in the city. Eleonora G. from the Arci tells "it all started with the space [...] people then pass by and see who's there and who's not, it's a point of reference." A second feature that helps providing grips to those experiencing landings regards the 'cross-ability' of spaces. We have discussed on a theoretical level and through empirical testimonies that landings imply a circular mobility (Tarrius, 1993). A clear example is that of seasonal workers, who stay in Palermo mainly during winter, waiting to find a job in the neighboring cities or regions. In these cases, supportive landing spaces are those that grant the access and use without asking for a willingness to stay, nor hindering a free exit. The design of the space can already express a degree of cross-ability. An example is that of the two doors of the Arci Porco Rosso and Ikenga, that are left open and which people cross in both ways to freely enter and exit. In the Missione dormitory, the low wall physically represents the low threshold – to be jumped over – of access and exit. The procedures that regulate access and exit play a key role in this regard: access requirements, booking and waiting procedures, but also the maximum length of stay count. The difference between public dorms and those of the Missione lies in these aspects; the former require an access interview and set a maximum stay of 30 days, while the latter guarantee direct access and do not control exits. In some cases, the concern about the temporariness and mobility of users has structured the service more deeply. This is the case of the STP clinics that, differently from other general clinics, give immediate answers to patients, documented and undocumented. A doctor of the STP clinic in the ARNAS Civico Hospital explains

> the point is that many cannot plan their departure, and this stresses the system. [...] What characterizes the clinic Aiuto Materno and mine is the release mode of the STP code: we issue them on sight. To migrants who are not in a reception center, you can't say 'come back in eight days,' so we do it right away and then start the procedure. Everything has to be done right away.

The same clinics also provide patients with a personal medical history notebook, with all data gathered from screenings and cares. The aim is to provide them with information that could be useful also elsewhere, acknowledging their right to movement. In other cases, procedures do not recognize the right to mobility of landing migrants and often imply a long permanence in the territory. This is the case of those offices and procedures that require several appointments and whose answers never arrive immediately, as for the municipal registration or, more generally, for the request of residence permits, even when temporary. Eleonora G. who accompanies migrants to the Municipal Registry Office, reports "they reached the point of fixing appointments at a year distance," and this of course does not match with the open temporality and mobility of landings. A third feature of landing spaces regards their accessibility and usability; as Doctor Gregorio M. states, "both access and usability must be guaranteed. For health clinics, it is not enough to be accessible, they must also be usable; there should be cultural mediators, schedules should allow people who work to use the clinic." The changing conditions of landings imply that people might have diverse competences of use of the territory and the degree accessibility and usability of spaces gains relevance. Accessibility often is defined on relative terms: the reciprocal position among spaces matters. The well-connected Casa dei Diritti is considered very

Urban spaces as landing infrastructures 127

far because is far from the networks of associations in Ballarò. Sara A. from Ikenga declares that the Casa dei Diritti "is too far away, it takes longer to bring someone there, than to try to solve any issue here." Additionally, for users, accessibility is not only measured on a distance base but also on the time availability, as the effectiveness of the Aiuto Materno health clinic shows.

The walk through these spaces highlights some common features that appear to be relevant for landing; however, when reporting these spaces on a map it emerges a relevant point: they present clear differences in terms of localization, dimensions, nature and functions. The actors and institutions involved, the service provided, the spaces and urban contexts are hardly comparable. In this sense, this gaze teaches us also that the geography of landing spaces defies conventional logics of welfare and urban planning. They not only exceed the limits of arrival neighborhoods but also belong to diverse government sectors and pop-up without following plans and programs. Nowadays, this consideration matches with a wider discourse, that underlines how many spaces of services nowadays do not follow the logics of distribution and localization on which planning is based and rather follow a pop-up dynamic (Bricocoli and Sabatinelli, 2018). In the last years across Europe, this was also very clear with reception systems, camps and facilities often opened where resources and spaces were available rather than as a result of planning choices. Against this background, the interim nature of landings, their unpredictable intensity over time and the multidimensional factors shaping migrants' journeys render the geography of landing spaces even harder to be grasped and addressed. This calls into question the role of planning when confronted to landings and these spaces, how to grasp and be aware of these geographies of spaces and actors, in the first place? And then, how to govern them and how to channel landing processes? Given the multiplicity of spaces, temporalities and actors involved, we may argue that the aims and modes of grasping and channeling landing processes urge to be discussed.

Finally, through the investigation on how landing spatializes, we may draw a third consideration about the relevance of the micro- and spatial dimension of landing infrastructures. The urban context matters, and the localization of spaces defined in absolute terms and in relation to other locations influences their degree of accessibility. The buildings that host the spaces observed also play a role, as 'containers' of landing spaces: the huge area of the Missione dorms, the big complex of the Immigration Office that hosts the smaller waiting area at the entrance gate, the ground floor rooms of the Arci Porco Rosso or the bigger heritage building of the Centro Astalli. Within these larger architectural structures, however, landing spaces are often more specifically defined through micro-spaces experienced by who lands. More than the whole urban context or building of the Immigration Office, we have seen how the waiting area on the sidewalk before the entrance gate is a core space in the experience of newcomers. Similarly, some of the STP clinics are located within larger hospital campuses that however are hardly mentioned nor experienced by newcomers. What emerges from the interview and the observation is the relevance of a micro-dimension of spaces that coincides with the experienced one. Landings seem to put and accent on this latter dimension of the micro-experienced space, more than the others and the material and immaterial organization of these waiting spaces, helpdesks, small squares or thresholds gains relevance. Measures, layout, openings and entrances play a relevant role in allowing or hindering the accessibility and usability of landing spaces.

Notes

1 All names of interviewees had been changed to preserve anonymity.
2 Historically, Biagio Conte would realize his protests and claims though prolonged fasting and bare-foot walks through the city.
3 The Municipality has recently widened the public dorm offer, thanks to European and PON (National Operative Program) funding. However, they overall offer approximately 200 beds. The access is not direct and requires the intermediation of an association notifying a person in need; one day a week, notified people are signed in for a meeting with the managing institution and a public social worker; only after this meeting, they can access dorms. Interestingly, dorms keep one bed for 'emergency cases,' that are allowed a direct access, if notified by associations; this gives a certain degree of flexibility to the system (Eleonora G., volunteer at Arci Porco Rosso helpdesk). These facilities are conceived as a 'pit-stop' solution (Valerio M., Opera Don Calabria), where people should reach a certain degree of autonomy; therefore, hosts are usually asked not to stay longer than 30 days – although they are allowed to go back to the dorm if needed. During the COVID-19 pandemic, these dorms were turned into day-and-night facilities, people were allowed to stay and new entrances were restricted to avoid the contagion. Generally, instead, these are only

night-facilities, and hosts are asked to leave dorms in the morning and go back before evening.
4 Arci is a cultural and social association, spread in the national territory through circles and associations. It was born in 1957 as an organization for the development of the *case del popolo* (Eng. houses of people) and recreative circles.
5 Francesco Bellina is a Palermitan photographer, who made interesting works connecting Ballarò and Nigeria following trafficking networks, his website is available at this link www.francescobellina.photoshelter.com (last accessed on September 30, 2021).
6 Astalli is a national wide Catholic organization, with centers spread in different Italian cities.
7 Healthcare clinics for foreigners historically were born in Palermo to answer the health demand of the first immigrants settling in the historic center, back in the 1980s; through advocacy actions and feedbacks at the institutional level, the involved doctors managed to shift the medical activity to the public sector, and open within the local Health Agency the Operative Unit specialized in foreign cares.
8 Interestingly, this public attention to migration medicine is a peculiarity of the Sicilian region where healthcare passed from being a mainly volunteering activity to the public sphere. Indeed, in other Italian regions until today, the main reference for migrant healthcare – especially for undocumented migrants – remain associations and STP clinics have a very reduced role.
9 Interestingly, this is also the potential workforce that was mentioned in Section 3.2.

References

Anderson, E. (2011) *The cosmopolitan canopy: Race and civility in everyday life*. New York and London: W.W. Norton.
Bifulco, L. (eds) (2003) *Il Genius Loci del welfare. Strutture e processi della qualità sociale*. Rome: Officina Edizioni.
Bricocoli, M. and Sabatinelli, S. (2018) "Città, welfare e servizi: temi e questioni per il progetto urbanistico e le politiche sociali," *Territorio*, 83, pp. 106–110. doi: 10.3280/TR2017-083015
Bully, É. (2022) *Palerme, «Ville Accueillante»? Instrumentalisation politique de l'accoglienza, formes d'hospitalité locale et effets sur les trajectoires des exilés*. Université Paris-Est.
Crosta, P. L. (2010) *Pratiche. Il territorio "è l'uso che se ne fa."* Milan: FrancoAngeli.
Crosta, P. L. (2018) "Territori," in Bifulco, L., Borghi, V., and Bricocoli, M. (eds.) *Azione pubblica. Un glossario Sui Generis*. Milan: Mimesis, pp. 145–150.

de Leonardis, O. (2001) *Le istituzioni: come e perché parlarne*. Rome: Carocci.

Fontanari, E. (2019) *Lives in transit: An ethnographic study of refugees' subjectivity across European borders*. London: Routledge.

Klinenberg, E. (2018) *Palaces for the people. How social infrastructure can help fight inequality, polarization, and the decline of civil life*. New York: Crown.

Lieto, L. (2022) "Planners as brokers and translators. On regulation and discretionary power," in Rydin, Y. *et al.* (eds.) *Regulation and planning. Practices, institutions, agency*. New York and Abingdon: Routledge, pp. 83–96.

Meeus, B. *et al.* (2020) "Broadening the urban planning repertoire with an 'Arrival Infrastructures' perspective," *Urban Planning*, 5(3), pp. 11–22. doi: 10.17645/up.v5i3.3116

Meeus, B., Arnaut, K. and van Heur, B. (2019) *Arrival infrastructures: Migration and urban social mobilities*. Springer International Publishing. doi: 10.1007/978-3-319-91167-0

Tarrius, A. (1993) "Territoires circulatoires et espaces urbains: Différentiation des groupes migrants," In: *Les Annales de larecherche urbaine*. N°59–60, 1993. Mobilités. pp. 51–60. doi: https://doi.org/10.3406/aru.1993.1727

Viani, G. (2019) "Alcune osservazioni etnografiche sulle comunità mauriziane induiste a Palermo (2009–2019)," *Dialoghi Mediterranei*, March. Available at www.istitutoeuroarabo.it/DM/10yearsmigrationchallenge-alcune-osservazioni-etnografiche-sulle-comunita-mauriziane-induiste-a-palermo-2009-2019/, last accessed on March 11, 2024.

Weick, K. E. (1995) *Sensemaking in organizations*. Thousand Oaks, CA: SAGE.

5 Working perspectives

When first addressing the topic of landing within an Architecture and Urban Studies Department, the main hypothesis was that these issues would introduce concerns and challenges that are relevant to these disciplines, even beyond the specificities of migrant newcomers' presence in cities. In fact, landing is not only an issue we urge to address *per se* but also an opportunity to think of alternatives for our cities and to reflect upon the tools that, as planners and architects, we have to contribute to this effort. Drawing on the debate on arrival, we will outline a long-term challenge and three fields of action and experimentation emerging from this work.

5.1 Rethinking the city starting from its uses

Before addressing some possible fields of action emerging from this work, we can underline the broader challenge that the discussion on landing introduces. Landing processes intrinsically question the way the city is thought and organized; thus in the first place, there is a need to recognize this challenge and to work on it in the long term. The debate on arrival strives to underline the complexity of this process, and the research on arrival experiences clearly shows how little this complexity is grasped and addressed by regulatory frameworks, tools and planning practices. The temporal, territorial and subjective experience of people on the move, upon arrival, clashes with planning rationales grounded on principles of permanence, stability and prevision, addressing and observing landings in border contexts, such as the Mediterranean ones, makes this clash even clearer. Landing processes express an 'interim' and intrinsically open condition, that

DOI: 10.4324/9781003441342-5

lies between the travel and settlement, how can we plan with and for this 'interim?'.

Working in this direction implies in the first place an intense political claim. As Meeus *et al.* (2020) recognize, their infrastructural perspective and the need of broadening futuring vectors "is of course also an intensely political statement as it seeks to facilitate an everyday 'right to the city,' building on the famous concept of Lefebvre (2009) [...]" (*ibidem*, p. 18). In Section 2.2.2, we have seen how Latham (2014) underlines that 'liberating temporariness' implies also "liberating permanence (as opposed to temporariness) as the sole basis of justice, rights, and security (broadly defined)" (*ibidem*, p. 25); it implies questioning the prevalence of permanence which the Western society has always favored, as a synonym of stability and certainty. Tarrius (1993) argues that the dualistic approach to sedentariness and mobility still informs societies and spaces, and he criticizes it through the introduction of the new understanding of territories as 'territories of circulation.' The concept of plural subjectivities and populations introduces similar concerns, and Pasqui (2008) underlines that this perspective not only questions the relation between political legitimacy, based on territorial sovereignty, and the variety of practices that define territories today but also the mechanisms of representation and identification of collective interests. Around migration processes, as seen, Crosta (2018) argues that our government system does not provide 'political space' to those who actually 'build' the territory through the use they make of it. Thus, dealing with a radically open-ended process, as landing, questions many of the dualistic paradigms Western society is based. It represents a battle for rights, based on an actual presence, in the 'here and now,' no matter what the future will bring next; a work on presence as a political tool that disrupts normative accounts of forced migration (Darling, 2017). Within this framework, the challenge of landing is also at the level of urban planning and policy practices. In a recent contribution to territorial research, Crosta and Bianchetti (2021) write that planning

> has always been intended as a form of prevision. The result of a culture based on prevision and development that hardly matches with the variety of rationalities at work on the territory [..] In so doing, planning approaches reality through lenses that reduce its indeterminacy.
>
> (*ibidem*, pp. 10–13)

These reflections refer to a broader crisis of planning but fit the case of migration processes and landings, where we witness a discrepancy between the variable nature of landing and the way the territory is organized and governed. The open-endedness of landing indeed mismatches with the categories and normativities through which planning aims at predicting and governing migration processes. In this sense, the effort shall be that of remaining open to indeterminacy, working on "a design approach that leaves sufficient room for 'uncertainty as a productive factor' (Havik, Patteeuw and Teerds, 2011, p. 4)" (Meeus *et al.*, 2020, p. 18). In fact, this invitation emerges from many of the contributions we have discussed; Latham (2014) himself writes that liberating temporariness implies insisting on a condition of indeterminacy, and Mehrotra and Vera (2015), in their work on ephemeral urbanism, argue that incompletion and spatial-temporal openness are central questions. In the literature on the territorial dimension, the major challenge is building the condition for openness to mobility. This challenge involves the planning practices on many levels: the way access to public housing is regulated often grounds on a long-term permanence requirement, and the way access to shelters is organized also implies a certain stability on the same territory. The criteria used to distribute and design welfare facilities often are shaped by fixed categories (resident, regular migrant..) of people. To see how the city could react 'otherwise' the examples discussed in Section 2.5 are inspiring and deploy through different dimensions – from the organizational to the spatial one. . As regards reception experiences, we mentioned the case of Grande-Synthe, where the spatial and administrative organization of the camp aimed at accommodating a greater diversity of futuring vectors for 'transmigrants,' recognizing the need to plan also for those who were not willing to stay and mixing the language of temporariness of these population with that of permanence of the infrastructures built for them. The Milanese reception hub, despite with very low-quality standards, was able to accommodate transiting migrants without requiring them to enter the Municipal reception system. Similarly, the low wall and loose protocols of the Palermitan private dorms ensured a convenient degree of 'crossability' for a space hosting seasonal workers in Sicily. These experiences differ a lot from those of reception facilities that only provide temporary structures to temporary migrants, often 'trapping' people on the move within national borders and grounding on a request of permanence on the same territory. We also encountered the example of public services that manage to support landing migrants through their organization: the SAIER in Barcelona, by adopting a broad definition of 'people on the move' – instead of legal categories – tries to build the conditions of access and usability for all populations living for a certain time in Barcelona. The health clinic investigated in Palermo successfully deals with newcomers with changing legal status and transiting migrants by providing immediate access to essential cares – working around a national system with much longer timings. Between the planning and architectural fields, we have seen how the design and organization of smaller spaces can indeed challenge more traditional rationales and support landings. The two doors of the Arci Porco Rosso helpdesk or the 'indoor public space' of the Centro Astalli create a welcoming environment and make thresholds very permeable also for people on the move.

Acknowledging the need to rethink the way the city is designed and organized also has a methodological implication; namely, adopting a 'phenomenological approach' able to learn from the way landing deploys on the field and from how the infrastructuring work already happens. In the recent presentation of the edited volume *TheoriSE, debating south-eastern turn in planning theories* (Yiftachel and Mammon, 2022), it was discussed that in situations where conventional planning categories hardly fit, there is a need to build a complementary planning vocabulary, and that to this aim, we should learn from places and practices that already embody an alternative. This invitation applies also to landing and landing infrastructures that often exceed traditional planning rationales and tools and that require to broaden the planning vocabulary, as suggested by Meeus *et al.* (2020). In this work, investigating the changing profiles of landing newcomers and unpacking their ways of using the city revealed how landing infrastructures support or hinder the everyday life of newcomers in Palermo. Only by getting to know the circular mobility of seasonal workers can we understand that accessibility is not enough, but a certain degree of 'crossability' is needed. Only by understanding the fragmented temporality of asylum seekers and the continuous change of legal status can we realize how the National health system is not always accessible to them. In this sense, this work firmly embraces the invitation for a place-based approach to the urban analysis of landing and landing infrastructures to grasp the field's dynamics and question if and how they can be embedded in the urban planning vocabulary.

5.2 Regulatory frameworks, public action and spaces

Once the primary and long-term challenge that landing introduces is clarified, we can outline some fields where this process can start. In all cases, what emerges as crucial is the presence of progressive – and sometimes very small – attempts to act otherwise. When moving within an unknown field, not only place-based knowledge but also progressive experimentation and learning experiences are crucial. All examples we have cited above, in fact, are attempts to act otherwise within the planning field. Many have a contradictory character and only provide partial or temporary solutions, and some strongly depend on the agency of individuals rather than grounding in a more structured setting. However, they all open possible ways toward a shift in our gaze and represent fruitful examples to imagine a more structural change. In this sense, we will highlight three fields of action that appear as possible starting points for experimentation to outline some working perspectives.

5.2.1 The invitation to open institutional settings and regulatory frameworks to indeterminacy

A first relevant theme, and possible field of action, regards the diverse forms of institutionalization and regulatory frameworks landing practices are caught in. Despite not being extensively addressed in this work, this issue represents a relevant underlying theme. We have seen how landing processes and the presence of newcomers on the territory deploy through complex forms that can be hardly grasped by existing governing categories; we have also seen how often resources and the infrastructuring work come 'from below' (Meeus et al., 2020), namely from places and actors that not necessarily belong to institutionalized settings, nor work within formalized regulatory frameworks. The different ways of institutionalization of landings are discussed in the debate on arrival and were mirrored throughout the research; on a translocal scale, we have seen how immigration policies, more specifically asylum and reception policies or local initiatives try to channel migration movements into rigid systems. Similarly, the sectorial way in which migration is often managed, with different institutions working on very separate fields – i.e. above all the legal, health and social ones – hinders and effective treatment of this multidimensional phenomenon both at a supralocal and local scale. In the planning field, some regulations within institutional settings are very rigid when it comes to embracing the indeterminacy of landing: Meeus *et al.* (2020) unpack how this rigidity is mirrored in public housing and shelter policies, requiring proof of long-term permanence or willingness for it, to grant access. Similarly, Schillebeeckx *et al.* (2019) underline how strict zoning mechanisms and rules hinder to fully value the role that certain places play for arrival – for instance, ethnic shops working also as social infrastructures. In this sense, the question arises how planning and policy, traditionally inscribed within institutional settings and producing regulatory frameworks can be developed to support landing and landing infrastructures.

Drawing from the experiences reported in this work, we can embrace a shared invitation to leave some space for indeterminacy within the planning practice. Still recognizing the need for planning disciplines to work with categories and within regulatory frameworks, the suggestion is to try and produce looser regulations, able to leave some space for the unknown and to learn from it. Authors claim for looser regulatory frameworks (Meeus *et al.*, 2020), a laissez-faire approach (Saunders, 2011), up to suggesting the need to include the frame of informality within the urban planning discourse (Fawaz, 2017; Cremaschi and Lieto, 2020). What we observed in Palermo helps us grounding this invitation. The case of the public and private dormitory offer, as well as the regulation of the Arci Porco Rosso helpdesk, shows that allowing for a certain degree of looseness is fruitful but not easy to realize. We discussed how the difference between the public and private dorms reveals a trade-off between quality and access that in that context remains largely unsolved. On the one hand, the strict access and staying procedures of the public facilities aim at granting some quality and however hinder the access to many landing migrants; on the other hand, private dorms granted high accessibility, and 'crossability,' to the price of quality. In this sense, experimentations as the one of the Milanese Hub (*see* Section 2.5.3) are insightful stories to look at. There, within an institutional setting, a certain degree of looseness was allowed, but only for a limited time period, with the help of a managing actor that was not the Municipality and based on the individual responsibility that a public officer took for that. Interestingly that limited experience became a learning opportunity for the Municipality later built on that to design a new reception space. Despite being very limited in time and space,

Working perspectives 137

these experiences show how complex it is to open institutional setting and regulatory frameworks to 'indeterminacy' and how necessary it is to learn from that. Limiting the timing of such experiences, involving different actors and counting on individuals' discretionary power and response capacities appear key ingredients for this.

5.2.2 Embracing a broad definition of 'public' action and recognizing the role of individuals' discretionary power

A second aspect to be addressed is that of the actors who are and should be involved in the definition of public action around landing and the related infrastructuring work. As reported in Section 3.2, I have been told to be ready for a broad definition of 'public action' when confronted with the Palermitan context; in fact, this invitation echoes a key topic of discussion in the debate on landing and landing infrastructures. Within this discussion, there are two aspects worth addressing. Firstly, there is a need to recognize the wide range of actors involved in the infrastructuring of landing; in Palermo, actors were of different kinds: more or less formalized associations, a lay priest managing the widest dorm offer in the city, a lively and local third sector next to a more established set of actors working very closely to the Municipality and the Municipality, constrained within structural limits and capacities of the public hand and a very open political discourse. In line with these observations, scholars underline that, in the face of the limitations of public institutions to address landings, the infrastructuring work largely happens 'elsewhere,' within more and less formalized networks of actors. This implies not only the need, from the planning and policy standpoint, to 'see' and recognize the role of these actors but also the urge to find ways to include them in the development of initiatives and policies addressing landing migrants. The housing and shelter domain is again very enlightening in this sense: in recent years, many projects dealt with the topic of access to housing for newcomers. However, many stuck to the modification of existing institutional tools, and fewer engaged with not-formalized and not-institutional solutions to housing provided by co-nationals in the private rental market. How to include these actors and experiences in the institutional effort of reception?

The work on Palermo reveals a further relevant aspect, namely the role that individuals play in addressing the indeterminacy of landing. Interestingly, independently from the type of context – is it more or less institutionalized – much of the infrastructuring work grounds on individual accountability and discretionary power of single actors in the field. The examples of the Police Immigration Office and the health clinic help in this sense. The first deals with landing migrants within a very rigid institutional system, which relates to a provincial and national level; everything, from the spatial layout to the procedures to the behaviors of operators and officers, confirms this institutional rigidity. The accessibility and usability of this place – as we defined them – are very low. Instead, the health clinic Aiuto Materno offers a different example: here despite being a public institution, the clinic does offer effective conditions of accessibility and use, as all the interviewees reckon. In this case, the agency and power of the two service managers, the doctor and the social worker, prove crucial; their discretionary power (Lieto, 2022) opens a space of possibility to interpret changing needs and build possible answers. They chose to modify opening hours, during the pandemic they explicitly asked the head of the provincial sanitary agency to stay open; they organized the space so to provide comfortable conditions for waiting. A similar case is that of the Casa dei Diritti, a public office that grounds its potential of accessibility and attractiveness on the agency of its operators. The shared pattern among the latter cases is the discretionary power of single actors within public institutions, who were in the position and chose to work around given directives to keep existing services and spaces accessible (Bovo, 2023). This was made possible by the improper use of procedures, the assumption of some risks and deviations from a given protocol – which at that moment required all public spaces to close; the subjectivity of these actors proved crucial, as well as their capacity to interpret and react to the context in which they work (de Leonardis, 2001). The case of the Arci Porco Rosso provides further food for thought, here indeed the accountability and individual choices of its founders and volunteers are always described as a crucial factor for its infrastructuring role for landing migrants. During the pandemic, a moment when the vulnerability of landing migrants increased, they managed to adapt quickly to the restrictions and the newly emerging needs. The space turned into a back office and food storage when front-office activities were forbidden, and, at the same time, volunteers kept in contact with 'users,' by everyday phone contacts. This range of developing reactions could be read through the concept of negative capability (Lanzara, 1993): in a condition of the resetting of conventional references, this reality managed to "institute a space of meaning, where actors could take a position and interact, starting the construction of new coordinates to define the situation, the framework and the actions" (de Leonardis, 2001, p. 134). Here again, existing norms were reinterpreted and shaped according to new emerging needs; this has been possible, thanks to a close connection to the territory and to the flexible structure of the third-sector associations. What these examples add to the debate is that not only is important to be aware and involve all stakeholders being part of an infrastructuring work but also to be aware that the agency – and power – of individuals within more or less institutionalized organizations proves crucial. In other words, building prepared territories for landing also implies investing on people and on their response capacities and not only in the services or spaces they work in.

5.2.3 Spaces as starting points for experimentation

The last field of action regards spaces intended both as physical settings and objects of organization. This work focused on the spatial dimension of landing infrastructures as a starting point and discussed how observing landing spaces is a way of grasping the nature of landing processes themselves. However, we may argue that spaces are also where experimentation and innovation can take place and are, therefore, fruitful tools for policy. In the cases we have encountered, 'innovation' and efforts of successfully infrastructuring landings mainly happened at a very local scale, rather than at a higher policy level. This is the case of the Arci Porco Rosso helpdesk and of the health clinic Aiuto Materno or the public helpdesk of Casa dei Diritti. In these cases, the attempt to better adapt to migrant's needs started from the opening and the setting up of a service in a space. In the health clinic Aiuto Materno, the disposal of material artifacts such as the bench, the way the entrance is organized, and the physical proximity between the social worker and the doctor are all tools to build a successful infrastructure. We may argue that, among other tools, spaces are indeed where policy development can start from: experimentation and learning opportunities. The infrastructuring work toward landing may indeed start from spaces, their layout and organization.

Further on this point, it is worth underlining that in most cases, what is mobilized is a micro-scale of design and planning, involving the interior setup rather than the construction of new physical infrastructures. In many cases, these landing spaces are within already existing structures that for a certain time work also for landing, as in the case of the Arci, the health clinic, the CLEDU helpdesk and many others. In this sense, the layout and the light organization of micro-spaces gain a central role in making sense of it in shorter time cycles, and the organizational dimension gains relevance over the more permanent design of space. Particularly, organization involves both the design and regulation of space and, thus, both material configurations and competencies needed to make sense of it (Weick, 1995; de Leonardis, 2001; Bifulco, 2003). In the first place, this calls into question the material dimension of organization; as seen in the field, spatial configurations help making a certain sense of a space, giving it a peculiar meaning – being it that of powerlessness and exclusion, or that of welcoming. While discussing this in a short conversation with Rahul Mehrotra,[1] he mentioned that from an architectural and planning design point of view, this is a crucial point. If we take a street and put lights in the shape of a canopy, it already creates some sense of festivity although in the next morning, when the lights are off, it will turn again into an ordinary street. In other words, the critical design question is how we use material deployment to create associations on smaller time cycles. What materials do we deploy to make a specific sense of a space and create association? How do we build a sense of refuge or a temporary sense of stability – even if not permanence? Against this background, it emerged also the relevance of 'interpretation competencies.' When it comes to organizing, or re-organizing, the spaces of the health clinic, what makes the difference is the ability of certain actors to interpret the situation and to react consequently. The organizational dimension of spaces also mobilizes an experience-based knowledge that is played out instantly. For disciplines that often work at an urban scale, on permanent spaces and regulating long-term transformations, grasping the relevance of this small scale and instant organizational dimension as a resource to address open and plural processes is not an easy task; however, this seems to be an urgent and core point to be aware of. In this sense, it is worth mentioning the work of Laura Lieto.[2] When reporting on research on health clinics of the NGO Emergency in Naples, she mentions that these realities bring into play a flexible way of producing services, a very light and fast way based on intermittency, as well as on the ability to turn relationships on and off, and have as a philosophy a radically cooperative model.

She underlines

> the peculiar way in which these subjects organize themselves in space, the clinics are, above all, linked on the one hand to the third sector and, on the other, to the NGOs of the humanitarian world. They are intermittent spaces, they come on and go off, they stay one period there and another here.

In synthesis, she adds that "organizational cultures count a lot in this model." We may argue that space is a setting, and the organizational dimension is central, in its material and immaterial components. Landing as an interim enhances the role of space in an organizational field (Weick, 1995; Czarniawska, 1997) and questions the kind of competencies needed for its deployment. In this sense, spaces become great opportunities for experimentation; the recognition of this dimension allows us also to value the role of urban planning and architecture in creating and supporting landing infrastructures.

Notes

1 Chair of the Department of Urban Planning and Design at Harvard and co-author of *Ephemeral Urbanism* (2015); interviewed online by the author on September 9, 2021.
2 Interviewed online by the author on September 9, 2020.

References

Bifulco, L. (ed.) (2003) *Il Genius Loci del welfare. Strutture e processi della qualità sociale*. Rome: Officina Edizioni.

Bovo, M. (2023) "Access to essential services. Migrants' landing during lockdown," in Armondi, S. *et al.* (eds.) *Cities learning from a pandemic: Towards preparedness*. London: Routledge, pp. 232–243. doi: 10.4324/9781003240983-18

Cremaschi, M. and Lieto, L. (2020) "Writing Southern theory from the global North. Notes on informality and regulation," *Equilibri*, 24, pp. 261–280.

Crosta, P. L. (2018) "Territori," in Bifulco, L., Borghi, V., and Bricocoli, M. (eds.) *Azione pubblica. Un glossario Sui Generis*. Milan: Mimesis, pp. 145–150.
Crosta, P. L. and Bianchetti, C. (2021) *Conversazioni sulla ricerca*. Rome: Donzelli Editore.
Czarniawska, B. (1997) *A narrative approach to organization studies*. Edited by Czarniawska, B. Thousand Oaks, CA: SAGE.
Darling, J. (2017) "Forced migration and the city: Irregularity, informality, and the politics of presence," *Progress in Human Geography*, 41(2), pp. 178–198. doi: 10.1177/0309132516629004
de Leonardis, O. (2001) *Le istituzioni: come e perché parlarne*. Rome: Carocci.
Fawaz, M. (2017) "Planning and the refugee crisis: Informality as a framework of analysis and reflection," *Planning Theory*, 16(1), pp. 99–115. doi: 10.1177/1473095216647722
Havik, K. M., Patteeuw, V. and Teerds, P. J. (2011) "Productive uncertainty: Indeterminacy in spatial design, planning and management/ Redactioneel: Productieve onzekerheid: Het onvoorziene in planning, ontwerp en beheer," *Oase: Journal for Architecture*, 85, pp. 3–6.
Lanzara, G. F. (1993) *Capacità negativa. Competenza progettuale e modelli di intervento nelle organizzazioni*. Bologna: Il Mulino.
Latham, R. (2014) "Temporal orders, re-collective justice, and the making of untimely states," in Vosko, L. F., Preston, V., and Latham, R. (eds.) *Liberating temporariness?: Migration, work, and citizenship in an age of insecurity*. Kingston: McGill-Queen's University Press, pp. 272–295.
Lefebvre, H. (2009) *Le droit à la ville [The Right to the City]*. 3rd editio. Paris: Economica/Anthropos.
Lieto, L. (2022) "Planners as brokers and translators. On regulation and discretionary power," in Rydin, Y. et al. (eds.) *Regulation and planning. Practices, Institutions, Agency*. New York and Abingdon: Routledge, pp. 83–96.
Meeus, B. et al. (2020) "Broadening the urban planning repertoire with an 'Arrival Infrastructures' perspective," *Urban Planning*, 5(3), pp. 11–22. doi: 10.17645/up.v5i3.3116
Mehrotra, R. and Vera, F. (2015) *Mapping the ephemeral megacity*. Berlin: Harvard South Asia Institute, Hatje Cantz Verlag.
Pasqui, G. (2008) *Città, popolazioni e politiche*. Milan: Jaka Book.
Saunders, D. (2011) *Arrival city: How the largest migration in history is reshaping our world*. London: Windmill Books.
Schillebeeckx, E., Oosterlynck, S. and de Decker, P. (2019) "Migration and the resourceful neighborhood: Exploring localized resources in urban zones of transition," in *Arrival infrastructures: Migration and urban social mobilities*. Springer International Publishing, pp. 131–152. doi: 10.1007/978-3-319-91167-0_6

Tarrius, A. (1993) "Territoires circulatoires et espaces urbains: Différentiation des groupes migrants," *Les Annales de larecherche urbaine*. N°59–60, 1993. Mobilités., pp. 51–60. doi: https://doi.org/10.3406/aru.1993.1727

Weick, K. E. (1995) *Sensemaking in organizations*. Thousand Oaks, CA: SAGE.

Yiftachel, O. and Mammon, N. (eds) (2022) *theoriSE: Debating the southeastern turn in urban theories*. Cape Town: African Centre for Cities.

Closing credits and acknowledgments

Landing processes and infrastructures, as part of migratory movements, represent a key feature of our times and our territories. Gabriele del Grande (2023) defines our century as the 'mobile' century, underling the intrinsic link between the act of migrating and our recent past, present and future. When addressing this theme, two aspects remain very relevant: recognizing the centrality of citizenship and right to the city and the commitment to act from within our disciplinary field, as researchers, planners and architects. On the first point, addressing migration and landing processes, today, means to question the relation between new inhabitants and the right to the city. Besides representing the main trigger of this work, this topic has continuously returned along the way: while building the theoretical framework, while hearing and reading about experiences of landings in Palermo, while visiting homeless dorms and while spending mornings in front of the Immigration Office, in the words of activists, migrants, professors and policymakers afterwards, when writing. This topic calls into question the relation between law and justice, the rule of law and power relations at stake; migration is a field where there are institutional norms that mine basic rights of people, and there is the need to introduce changes and find new norms able to protect these rights. Secondly, I believe that to seriously contribute to build an 'otherwise,' it is necessary to clarify what our disciplinary competences and tools are and committing to mobilize them – avoiding universalistic forms of knowledge. As Lo Piccolo (2013) argues, addressing this topic implies, in our disciplines, being concerned with the effects of planning actions on it. Migration and landings force to a continuous confrontation between the theoretical available tools and the actual contexts where to mobilize them, where priorities need to be set and choices to be consequently made. I will keep questioning how to deal with this confrontation and I am grateful to this research, and to the people and spaces I encountered along the way, to have tirelessly reminded me the importance of keeping this issue in mind.

Finally, this work has been a space of experience, reflection and discovery, and I want to thank those who made it possible. In the first place, those who followed and supported its development as a PhD thesis at Politecnico di Milano: Gabriele Pasqui and Massimo Bricocoli, my supervisor and co-supervisor, and Paola Briata, the third co-supervisor of this work. I want to thank all the people, inside and outside the university, who have been willing to share their thoughts even when the ideas were still very embryonic: Bruno Meeus, Howard Duncan, Yvonne Franz, Rahul Mehrotra, Marco Cremaschi, Alessandro Balducci, Luca Gaeta, Antonella Bruzzese, Carlotta Fioretti and Tuna Tasan-Kok. This work takes shape from the words and experiences of the people it speaks of, all of whom I sincerely thank. Receiving time and testimonials opens the mind. Getting up close and personal with the lives of those facing our present and its issues has been a tremendous opportunity.

References

del Grande, G. (2023) *Il secolo mobile. Storia dell'immigrazione illegale in Europa*. Milan: Mondadori.
Lo Piccolo, F. (2013) *Nuovi abitanti e diritto alla città: un viaggio in Italia*. Florence: Altralinea Edizioni.

Index

Note: Page numbers in *italic* refers to Figures.

accessibility 3, 98, 104, 126–8, 134, 136, 138; conditions of 37, 50–1; degree of 126–7, 138
agency 39, 122; Health 111–12, 129; individual xi; of migrants' 6, 20
anthropology 3
architecture 3, 5, 6, 22, 28, 46, 141; collective 45–6; Department of 1, 131; Exhibition 2
Arci 93, 96, 98, 102, 117
assemblages 5
asylum 2, 18, 25, 48, 67, 69, 71, 85, 105, 134; centers 21; crisis 2; policies 26; request 67, 69, 71, 101, 111; seekers 3–4, 6, 18, 39–40, 43–4, 49–50, 67, 74–5, 79, 134

border regime 40, 64

circular 12, 71; migration 16; mobilities 24, 32, 35, 48, 85, 93, 125, 134; territories 36
contested mobilities 62
COVID-19: crisis 37; outbreak 8; pandemic 8, 113, 118, 128; restrictions 100

design 6, 30, 45–6, 123, 125, 133–4, 136, 139–40; architectural 46; incremental 30; interior 3; urban 28
destination 14, 17, 22, 33, 69, 72
direct observation 7–8
discretionary power 124
diversity 3, 19–20, 39, 133
dormitory 125, 136
Dublin Regulation 71

ephemeral urbanism 28–9, 133
ethnography 6; auto- 24

fieldwork 6–8, 18
fragmented temporalities 38, 85, 111, 134

ground floor 94–6, 113, 117–18, 128

healthcare 97, 112, 116; system 70

immigration office 77, 100–1, 104–5, *106, 108*, 110–11, 119, 128, 138
indeterminacy 28, 132, 135–7
informality 136
institutional: learning 135–6, 139; settings 135–6
interim 29, 127, 131–2, 141
interviews 7, 18, 97, 105

Index 147

knowledge 6, 23, 42; collective 34; experience-based ix, 140; forms of x; -gain 21; kind of xi; place-based 135; situated x, 125

laissez-faire 136
looseness 104, 116–17, 123–4, 136

maps x, 7, 22, *64*

neighborhoods 13–15, 20, 36, 78, 93, 99, 101; arrival 2, 14–15, 20, 78, 87, 127; destitute 14; Eritrean 31; ethnic 3; marginalized 68; peripheral 97; popular 77–8; urban 20
normative xi, 44; categories 33, 50; handbooks 22; manuals xi; system 5

organizational: cultures 141; dimension 140–1

permanent-temporary: binaries 24, 30, 47; nexus 26
phenomenological approach 6, 134
pilot books x, 12, 22
place-based 6, 9, 44, 134–5
plurality 17, 39, 42–3, 125
port of first entry 13
public action 75, 135, 137

qualitative 7

regulatory frameworks 44–5, 131, 135–7
resourcefulness 14, 78

safe country 69, 71, 85
seasonal: jobs 94; work 85; workers 125, 133–4
sedentary-mobile: binaries 47
sketches 7, 120
sociology 13
spatialization 4–5, 77
specialization 13–14, 98, 110, 112, 122; functional 104; physical 111
subjectivity 19–20, 39–41, 138
support networks 14, 21, 33, 78, 86

temporality 19, 22–3, 30, 35, 38, 85, 97, 127, 134
territoriality 31, 35
third-sector 48, 74, 75–7, 102, 139
transition 13–14, 32
transmigrants 36, 47, 133
Tunisia 66–8

uncertainty 7, 22, 34, 133
undocumented 18, 116, 126; life 71; migrants 50–1, 70, 118, 125; people 111; workers 24

visibility 3, 95, 104

For Product Safety Concerns and Information please contact our EU representative GPSR@taylorandfrancis.com
Taylor & Francis Verlag GmbH, Kaufingerstraße 24, 80331 München, Germany

www.ingramcontent.com/pod-product-compliance
Lightning Source LLC
Chambersburg PA
CBHW051749230426
43670CB00012B/2211